ABOUT

Managing money is not just a technical exercise, but a spiritual discipline. There is an active power behind money which Jesus unmasked and called 'mammon.' He told his followers in strong terms that, "You cannot serve both God and Mammon."

We all manage money on a daily basis. Jesus is saying that mammon is a power behind money which wants to lead us away from God's ways of handling money. How does mammon affect our financial decisions? How can the influence of mammon be overcome? How can we use our money in a way that God would want us to?

This book is all about managing our money wisely. The monkey is 'mammon,' a tricky, unruly creature who is constantly seeking to destroy our relationship with God and our neighbour!

Money, mammon & the monkey uses the parable of Jesus, told in Luke, chapter 16 and verses 1 to 15, called in many translations 'The Unjust Steward.' This book will explain how his master called the steward 'shrewd,' and how we can deal 'shrewdly' with money in all our daily affairs.

THE AUTHOR

Peter Briscoe an Englishman, born in 1950, and studied Industrial Chemistry and Management at Loughborough University of Technology. He moved to The Netherlands in 1974 and was asked by his company to set up a subsidiary in Holland, selling chemical specialties to the aerospace and food processing industries. From 1986 to 2002, Peter was Executive Director of CBMC, Christian Businessmen's Committees, in Holland.

In 1990, Peter set up "Synthesys". a consulting company specialising in chemical product development. When the Berlin Wall collapsed in 1990, Peter developed Europartners, a movement dedicated to reaching European business and professional leaders for Christ.

From 2002, Peter took an assignment as Managing Director of HE Space Operations, serving the European Space institutions, specialising in providing professional services for spaceflight activities.

From 2008, Peter retired from business to develop a movement of Biblical stewardship in Europe, first of all through Crown Financial Ministries and then Compass - finances God's way.

At home, Peter is Chair of the Church board of the Baptist Church of Leiden. He is married to his Dutch wife, Didie since 1972. They are blessed with three daughters and six grandchildren.

September 2023 Edition 3

ISBN: 9789083228563

Published by: Compass - finances God's way
European office: www.compass1.eu

DEDICATION

This book is dedicated to the beloved women in my life.

To the memory of my late mother, who always called me 'a cheeky monkey.'

To my dear wife who is always telling me to stop monkeying around.

To my three daughters with whom we have more fun than a cartload of monkeys!

FOREWORD TO MONEY, MAMMON & THE MONKEY

About a third of Jesus' words were spoken in parables and about half of these had to do with money and possessions. In this book, Peter Briscoe sets about to inspire us from one parable which is one of the most difficult to understand. His novel approach to Jesus message on stewardship of the resources entrusted to us has certainly inspired me! Since I started on the topic of Biblical stewardship in 1974 and developing first Crown Ministries and then Compass - finances God's way, I am constantly surprised at how many new and unique ways God teaches me to manage money and possessions - His way!

Peter Briscoe is surely qualified to speak in the subject. He has been a leader in stewardship teaching in Europe for decades, and most importantly, he has lived and practiced what he preaches! He has been a respected business leader in the chemical and space exploration industries, combining his faith in Christ with business acumen. Peter has pioneered many Christian organisations involved in stewardship, serving churches, businesses and the public with innovative approaches to solve everyday problems and to help people grow in their faith!

This book will challenge your thinking about your own responsibilities as a faithful steward. Managing money is not merely a technical exercise, but also a spiritual discipline. This book is entered around Jesus unequivocal statement, "You cannot serve both God and mammon!" Most Bible translations render what Jesus called 'mammon' as money or wealth. In this book, Peter shows that there is much more depth to the word mammon than just money. He describes a power behind money which is diametrically opposed to God and which competes for our allegiance. The monkey in this book is mammon and in a humorous way, Peter describes how the clever monkey tries to trick us in ignoring Gods ways and in using people instead of serving them.

Peter gives very practical ways in which to become shrewd managers of Gods resources, using money to benefit people, helping them to enjoy Gods Kingdom.

I can heartily recommend 'Money, mammon & the monkey' for all followers of Jesus who want to grow in financial discipleship and generosity.

Howard Dayton, founder and CEO,
Compass - finances God's way.

CONTENTS

WILLIAM BLAKE, MAMMON.[1]

I rose up at the dawn of day—
'Get thee away! get thee away!
Pray'st thou for riches? Away! away!
This is the Throne of Mammon grey.'

Said I: This, sure, is very odd;
I took it to be the Throne of God
For everything besides I have:
It is only for riches that I can crave.

I have mental joy, and mental health,
And mental friends, and mental wealth;
I've a wife I love, and that loves me;
I've all but riches bodily.

I am in God's presence night and day,
And He never turns His face away;
The accuser of sins by my side doth stand,
And he holds my money-bag in his hand.

For my worldly things God makes him pay,
And he'd pay for more if to him I would pray;
And so you may do the worst you can do;
Be assur'd, Mr. Devil, I won't pray to you.

Then if for riches I must not pray,
God knows, I little of prayers need say;
So, as a church is known by its steeple,
If I pray it must be for other people.

He says, if I do not worship him for a God,
I shall eat coarser food, and go worse shod;
So, as I don't value such things as these,
You must do, Mr. Devil, just as God please.

---

1 The Poetical Works. 1908

INTRODUCTION 

One of the most memorable training sessions that I ever experienced as a young manager, was a very funny session led by John Cleese of Monty Python fame. We were all laughing as John Cleese sketched a situation of a manager trying to balance all the different responsibilities and tasks that he was assigned to. I'm sure you remember back at the circus where a Juggler tries to spin plates on about 12 sticks at the same time. Many managers feel just like this as they try to juggle all of the different tasks they have. In this training to learn how to delegate, John Cleese was working at his desk in an office with a monkey on his shoulder. And it was a very cheeky monkey.

The monkey represented a task which could easily be delegated. The manager could not keep the monkey from his back, and as soon as he tried to pass the monkey to somebody else, the monkey was clever and agile and, in every situation, jumped back onto the very tired manager's back. In the course of his job, he collected quite a few monkeys which wreaked havoc in the office - hammering on the keyboard, throwing the phone around, jumping on cupboards and swinging from the ceiling lamp.

The first people to write about this were William Oncken and Donald West in their classic 1974 article in the Harvard business review, who described a situation to open the eyes of the modern leader. The article was called, 'Who's got the monkey?' In this article the authors told about an overworked manager who allowed his subordinates to delegate everything upwards. When a manager takes an unsolved problem over from his subordinates, he allows a virtual monkey to jump off the back of the subordinate onto the back of the manager. This burden becomes heavier and heavier and he denies his people the chance to solve their own problems, thereby growing in the process.

I read a really good book by John Blanchard, called 'The One Minute Manager Meets the Monkey.' The lesson was the same, learning to delegate tasks, so that the burden falls from your shoulders and the task is done by somebody else who is more competent. That should be the secret to successful management - delegating the tasks which could be done by someone else and keeping time and energy to do tasks which most effectively could be done by yourself.

In this book I would like to introduce you to a spiritual monkey, a monkey which fastens itself to your back, which sits on your shoulder and which is intelligent and quick. This monkey works through your finances, predominantly focused on money and possessions. When this monkey is on your back he tries to manipulate every situation to get what he wants and eventually becomes a very heavy burden and an irritating pest. Jesus called this monkey 'mammon.' We need to learn to get the monkey off our backs, to be able to focus on Gods ways of handling money and possessions, to be able to serve God and not mammon.

This book offers a process of freeing you from that tricky monkey on your back, to be able to use money for God's purposes and to the benefit of your neighbour. This book is a plea that Christians learn to live and work in victory over mammon, who tries to disrupt our relationships, make us focus on materialism and ultimately serve his purposes. Mammon is alive and kicking! Jesus radically stated, "You cannot serve both God and mammon.' This book wants to help you to become free from this mischievous monkey.

Luke tells us a story about monkey business. The manager has a terrible job. He's the representative of the richest guy in town and has to deal with all sorts of money-hungry merchants and traders. The manager must combine the slippery skills of a politician, with the money savvy of an investor who trades in commodity futures. If he pours too much of his master's money in olive oil or wheat, and it's a bad year, then he'll be out of a job. And back then there aren't many second chances —mess it up, you're done, you spend the rest of your life among the expendable class, the beggars and common labourers. There isn't really another company or investment group to work for in town.

But apparently, our friend the manager offends some of the town traders enough for them to send some nasty rumours to the boss. They want the manager sacked; or maybe it's just the merchants showing their strong arm to the manager—letting him know who's really in charge.

I think we misunderstand this story if we conceive of the manager as dishonest, a thief, stealing from his boss. That's not what this story is about. This story is about a guy stuck right smack in the middle of an unjust, dog-eat-dog system. And the Bible translators lead us astray when they call the manager "dishonest". He is not. The Greek word is 'adikia'—and it means unjust, or unrighteousness. And he is not an unjust or unrighteous manager—he is the manager of unrighteousness, which is very different.

But what does that mean—to be a manager of unrighteousness? It means that he's caught in the middle of an unjust economic world, a world that operates in unrighteousness, a system that charges interest and creates severely burdened debtors in violation of God's law. What does the manager do? How does he manage all this unrighteousness?

The story goes …

> Luke recorded this parable, as told by Jesus, in the Bible, chapter 16.

> [1] He also said to the disciples, "There was a rich man who had a manager, and charges were brought to him that this man was wasting his possessions. [2] And he called him and

said to him, 'What is this that I hear about you? Turn in the account of your management, for you can no longer be manager.' ³ And the manager said to himself, 'What shall I do, since my master is taking the management away from me? I am not strong enough to dig, and I am ashamed to beg. ⁴ I have decided what to do, so that when I am removed from management, people may receive me into their houses.' ⁵ So, summoning his master's debtors one by one, he said to the first, 'How much do you owe my master?' ⁶ He said, 'A hundred measures of oil.' He said to him, 'Take your bill, and sit down quickly and write fifty.' ⁷ Then he said to another, 'And how much do you owe?' He said, 'A hundred measures of wheat.' He said to him, 'Take your bill, and write eighty.' ⁸ The master commended the dishonest manager for his shrewdness. For the sons of this world are more shrewd in dealing with their own generation than the sons of light.

⁹ And I tell you, make friends for yourselves by means of unrighteous wealth, so that when it fails they may receive you into the eternal dwellings.

¹⁰"One who is faithful in a very little is also faithful in much, and one who is dishonest in a very little is also dishonest in much. 11 If then you have not been faithful in the unrighteous wealth, who will entrust to you the true riches? ¹² And if you have not been faithful in that which is another's, who will give you that which is your own? ¹³ No servant can serve two masters, for either he will hate the one and love the other, or he will be devoted to the one and despise the other. You cannot serve God and money."

¹⁴ The Pharisees, who were lovers of money, heard all these things, and they ridiculed him. ¹⁵ And he said to them, "You are those who justify yourselves before men, but God knows your hearts. For what is exalted among men is an abomination in the sight of God.

For many Christians in business this is a strange story. Having your boss praising you for giving such hefty discounts, and giving a lot of money away? This looks like a monkey business - an unlikely story! I do not want to be irreverent, but I am a down-to-earth businessman - and you simply do not do that. What does Jesus want to tell us from this practical story? It is a case with which the brightest students of Harvard would have trouble finding the meaning!

The writer, Luke, was a doctor, a Greek and living right in the middle of society. He listened carefully to the testimonies of people who traveled around with Jesus and accurately reflected Jesus' words in accordance with his scientific education. In his book, Luke describes Jesus' teaching about money, wealth, and possessions, more than any other single topic. Our case is in the midst of a number of similarities and encounters around a similar theme.

In chapter 12, Jesus met two brothers, in conflict over the will of their father, both eager for the inheritance and Jesus tells a story of a rich fool, a successful businessman who was driven to great and better things and enjoying his abundance, without having an eye for the well-being of his soul and his eternal destiny.

In chapter 14, Jesus is invited to a dinner by a rich Pharisee. Jesus breaks all the rules of the protocol! He tells his host how to organise a party and how he should behave! Then he began to speak about God's banquet in the Kingdom of God with some poignant comments about the fact that some are too busy or too rich to take God seriously.

Chapter 15 contains penetrating stories about what it means to be lost, first on the basis of a lost sheep and a lost coin, and then of a lost son. This son claimed the inheritance, left the family business and wasted his fortune in a loose life abroad. Jesus' listeners are financial and religious professionals.

Chapter 16 begins with our manager accused of waste and ends with the rich man and poor Lazarus. One a very rich man who 'celebrated splendidly' every day and the other a beggar - sick, weak and rejected.

In chapter 17 we get a reminder of what happened in the days of Noah and Lot in Sodom and Gomorra. Both lived in times of material prosperity, but also in times of moral decay. It is necessary, told Jesus, that people who are busy becoming rich should also focus on peace with God in the light of God's judgment.

In chapter 18 we see another Pharisee and a tax collector together. They pray in the Temple. The Pharisee prides himself on giving the tithes, and the tax collector is aware of his unfair practices. Jesus meets a rich young leader who does not want to renounce his wealth.

In chapter 19, Jesus meets a tax inspector in Jericho who desires to meet Jesus and is radically converted.

Our story is right in the middle of a series of lessons and perhaps our difficult case study is a kind of hinge around which these stories and encounters revolve. Jesus spoke clearly and without hesitation about money because he was aware of the destructive effect in human lives and relationships. Our case has a special place because he made the cause of the temptations clear to us - mammon, our monkey!

Jesus told this story about what happened once upon a time in a large agricultural business enterprise. The main character in the parable is an economist, Greek 'oikonomos' = the administrator of the house. The master and owner of the business, a rich man, lives abroad. He owns an estate within the borders of Israel. The management of this is the responsibility of the steward, the manager of the farm. The steward must ensure that the business is run correctly and the profits are good. In this case, however, the situation is quite different.

Agricultural practices provided a framework for the lives of many Ancient Israelites. It's no accident that the Bible is filled with farming and land references and metaphors—most people were immersed in this work. Biblical stories reveal the relationship between Israelites, the land, and God. The agricultural practices of the Ancient Israelites reflected their understanding of themselves as stewards of land that was both a divine inheritance and a divine gift, but that the land ultimately belonged to God. God tells them, "No land may be permanently bought or sold. It all belongs to me—it isn't your land, and you only live there for a little while[2]"

One main reason for our problems with the parable is the great cultural distance separating us from the Mediterranean world of 2000 years ago. Some of the customs and values of the Messiah's day differ significantly from those of modern Western societies. We will look at some of these customs and values. For example, the importance of honour and shame in the Mediterranean culture of Jesus' day is one of those key cultural differences. A master's standing in the eyes of his peers was partly determined by his ability to control those under him. A master whose assets were wisely managed by a loyal steward would have been viewed highly by others. On the other hand, the misdeeds of an employee would have resulted in a loss of honour for the master. This plays an important role in our parable.

The Parable of the Shrewd Manager

The parable of Jesus in Luke 16 is indeed open to many interpretations. Mine is not from a theologian, but from an entrepreneur who, from the practice of doing business, makes an honest attempt to inspire the reader to follow God's ways, hand in hand with Jesus!

I was encouraged by Midrashim, which is the teaching method used by rabbis for centuries already. This means something like researching or looking for. The Jewish rabbis looked at Bible stories, tried to determine the meaning for their own life and times, and then they would develop other stories to illustrate and better understand the teaching, to fill in the gaps. Collections of such stories are part of the tradition which is passed down to future generations and which are used to illustrate teachings in the synagogue.

Thus, by 'filling the gaps', the rabbis showed that they were endowed by God with both a living imagination and a clear understanding of His ways and revelation through word and creation. They made

---

2 Leviticus 25:23

contemporary analogies, took the Biblical concepts and said, "Let me put it this way …" to revive old stories.

Jesus used this method in telling parables, and storytelling takes an important place in Jewish tradition. This truly Jewish way of telling has inspired me to let my imagination run its course, while I try to remain faithful to the Biblical interpretation.

Perhaps the reader will find something that raises disagreement or doubt. That is not bad at all. Feel free to ask questions in my interpretation. The Midrashim does not insist that only one interpretation is the right one.

Some theologians say that you should not take Jesus' parables apart and analyse them verse-by-verse for the applications. I am not a theologian, but spent more than 40 years in business. I know some wise sayings when I see them, and I can certainly be inspired by every word in the Bible! For an extensive theological treatment of the parable, I can refer the reader to the articles and books in the appendix.

Keys to the story

Our story was written down by Luke, a physician who wrote his account of what Jesus said in 'Koine Greek'. This Greek was simply the common language of the Mediterranean world in the first century. As Alexander the Great conquered the civilised world of his time, he spread Greek language and culture. Much like English has become today, Koine Greek became the most common and pervasive 'international language' of the day. Since most people could understand Koine, it was uniquely suited to proclaim the gospel throughout the world.

Not only was Koine Greek common in the sense it enjoyed widespread usage throughout the Roman Empire, but it was also common in the sense that it was not the language of the intellectual and academic elites. Classical Greek was used by the educated class. Koine Greek was the language of the working man, the peasant, the trader, and the housewife. This was the language of the New Testament and God wanted to make His words available to all, not just an elite few. There are six Greek words which are, in my opinion, essential to understand our story.

1. 'Oikonomos,' meaning an economist or steward. He is the manager of the rich man's farms. The story is about stewardship, using another's wealth wisely.

2. 'Methistemi,' meaning to change place, to remove from one place to another. The manager is being removed from his job and this is an allusion to when we will be removed from this earth to face our Maker. The story is essentially eschatological, concerned with our eternal destiny.

3. 'Phronimos,' meaning shrewd. The manager used practical wisdom to navigate a delicate situation and was praised for being shrewd and doing the right thing. The story is about showing practical wisdom in a tough situation.

4. 'Adikia,' meaning unrighteous. The Greeks had a goddess of injustice and wrongdoing called Adikia. It denotes a spirit of iniquity, always moving people to do wrong. The manager is called 'the manager of 'adikia'. And money is referred to as 'the mammon of 'adikia'. The story is about doing what is right and managing this all-present force which tends to dishonesty and to do what is wrong, unrighteous.

5. 'Mammonas,' meaning... mammon, (our monkey), the fallen spirit behind money which wants us to place our trust in money to bring us meaning and significance in life. In our story many Bible translators have translated this away as 'money' or 'wealth', neglecting the name 'mammon' which is a spiritual force diametrically opposed to God.[3] The story is essentially spiritual, about the choice we make to serve God or to serve mammon. We cannot do both.

---

3   Matthew 6:24

6. *'Pistos,'* meaning faithful. The manager was faithful in the transaction of his business, and the discharge of his duties, showing he is, in fact, trustworthy. The story is about faithfulness.

In short , we could re-tell our story in these two short sentences.

The steward (oikonomos), has to manage an unrighteous (adikia) financial situation and must correct it because he is being transferred (methisthemi) to another state. He devises a wise (phronimos), praiseworthy solution, faithfully (pistos) using unrighteous money (mammon of adikia) to make friends who will be introduced to Gods eternal home.

I choose to call our story, "The Parable of the Shrewd Manager." He is not the 'unrighteous steward', but the 'steward of unrighteousness'. He has to manage money which is the 'mammon of unrighteousness', ('mammonas tes adikias') and in this he is praised because he acted wisely.

Mammon, the fallen devil, the spirit behind money, couples with adikia, the spirit of iniquity to make the steward's life, and indeed our lives, very troublesome indeed! To manage this monkey - the mammon of adikia, you really need to be shrewd!

The Archbishop of Canterbury, Justin Welby wrote about the importance of this topic. "Mammon is so powerful that an attack on his authority over our lives, attitudes and thinking is as good a way of preparation for the reality of the Passion and crucifixion as I can imagine[4]."

The Bible on money

This book is all about handling money and possessions, God's way.

When we open the Bible, we do not find a philosophy, a political statement, a metaphysic or even a religion. We find instead the

---

4   "Dethroning Mammon" by Justin Welby, 2017

invitation for a dialogue, wherein God addresses a personal word to me, asking me what I am doing, hoping, fearing-and especially who I am.

All that the Bible has to tell me about money is found in this dialogue. It offers no objective discovery on which to base a general system. No formula for success can be found. Instead, it offers truth about all things, including money. This truth is found in relationship with Jesus and knowing the Bible, and nowhere else. Jesus said, "If you hold to my teaching, you are really my disciples. Then you will know the truth, and the truth will set you free." No amount of money will ever set us free; only in learning what the Bible teaches us about money and possessions can we enter into the freedom which Jesus offers. It is useless to try to extract from the Bible a money system applicable to the world, because people will recognise this truth only after they have come to faith.   The immense body of revelation, which contains, among other things, wisdom about money, does not appeal to reason, evidence or pragmatism; indeed, it is shut tight against these modes of conviction.

When looking at biblical passages about money, then, we must let them have the character God has given them. They are there because their content refers to God's work in Jesus Christ and our relationship to Him; we cannot take them out of this context.

These passages have to do with the relation between God and man. They are based on the personal relationship that is fundamental to the whole work of salvation; therefore, we cannot abstract them from a general idea, applicable to the world. They challenge us to commit ourselves. They start us down a certain path. They are not providing us with rational options or objective conclusions; the biblical texts never come to conclusions, because there is no conclusion apart from the heavenly Jerusalem and our resurrection.

The Biblical texts never provide "a solution." To the contrary, they get us started on a journey, and the only answer we can hope to find is, the one we ourselves give by our lives as we proceed on that journey.

Almost half of Jesus' parables tell about stewardship, using money and possessions. I think that Jesus talked so much about this because the concepts are so hard to understand.

They say basically three things about the steward … Firstly, about me; I was bought with a price and am not my own; secondly, about my things, my possessions. The thing about life is that it's not about things! Thirdly, it's about my thing … what I do with my things!

Jesus' parables about stewardship tell us six overarching lessons.

1. Someone is appointed to a position by a master and this position is a privilege, an honour not to be misused.

2. Emphasis is placed on how well the assigned responsibilities are carried out. The steward is put in charge to make it happen - work it!

3. There is an evaluation as to how well the responsibilities are carried out - whether the steward is (un)just, (un) faithful, or (un) wise.

4. The boss was not there to look over their shoulder. He gave an assignment and then disappeared. The steward was free to decide how he wanted to fulfil the assignment.

5. The steward was always tempted to use the position for his benefit, mistreating people or defrauding for own benefit.

6. There was a frequent reminder of a final reckoning to come, one day. The overseer will be brought to account. The steward often acts like this will never happen.

In this book, we will look at a strange parable, often called "The Unjust Steward." I believe the steward was not unjust, but cleverly managed a tough situation. I prefer to call it, "The Shrewd Steward." This has puzzled many people, theologians and business people alike, throughout the ages. I do not pretend to have all the wisdom on this topic but in this book, I will present my interpretation of the story. Enjoy the journey as we travel together through this story.

MONKEYNOMICS

Luke 16:1 Jesus told his disciples: "There was a rich man whose manager was accused of wasting his possessions."

The Monkey

I listened to an interesting presentation by Laurie Santos, head of a research institute at the Yale University that compares irrationality in humans and monkeys. Now I am certainly not in favour of the theory of evolution that we humans are descewndants of monkeys. (I like to believe the other way around, that monkeys are somehow devolved from people!)

She starts her presentation (from the series TED talks)[1] with the remark that people are extremely smart, but that we are also incredibly stupid when it comes to aspects of our decision-making. We think, she says, that the economic mistakes in the world are the fault of a few rotten apples or one of a few stupid, wrong decisions. But what social scientists are learning is that most of us, in certain circumstances, are going to make very specific mistakes. Those errors are predictable. We make them over and over again.

Where do these errors come from?

---

1   http://www.ted.com/talks/laurie_santos.html

Laurie Santos and her team, taught monkeys how to deal with money! She looked for the roots of human irrationality by looking at the way primates make decisions. A clever series of experiments in what she termed 'monkeynomics' shows that the stupid choices we make are also made by monkeys. She concluded that nothing has changed in 35 million years of evolution! Even if you don't have confidence in the theory of evolution, you have to conclude that monkeys and humans have many of the same qualities. Examples of this are irrational decision-making and the repetition of errors. Laurie Santos said that we have to learn to stay within our limits, and to use our creativity to solve problems. Our monkey, mammon, certainly uses our propensity for making stupid decisions which we later regret; certainly so in our financial dealings!

Well, we certainly have a complex problem scenario in our parable!

The Rich Man

The first character is introduced as a 'rich man.' Anyone who had a steward in those days would certainly be rich. By explicitly calling him 'rich' (Greek: *plousios*) Jesus was calling attention to the fact that the rich in Jesus' days were stereotypically despots, treating people poorly, exercising their power over those dependent on them. A word study of Luke's gospel affirms this. '*Plousios*' occurs many times. All those depicted as rich in these texts, are in one form or another excluded from the redeemed community or strongly disapproved of, with the single exception of the reformed Zacchaeus. The Palestinian hearer would certainly think of someone called '*plousios*' in a negative way. 'Woe to you who are rich, for you have received your reward[2].' Jesus called a rich man who was very successful in business a 'fool'[3], and described a hellish destination for a rich man who neglected the poor[4]. Paul exhorted Timothy to teach those who are rich, not

---

2   Luke 6:24
3   Luke 12:16
4   Luke 16:19

to trust in their riches[5] and James motivated the rich to be humble and realise the fleeting nature of his riches.[6] The rich in Laodicea are portrayed as being poor, wretched and blind.[7]

One of the ways mammon uses money and possessions is to enslave us in habits which are tough to break. Jesus told of how difficult it is for a rich man to enter the Kingdom of heaven[8] and how the antidote to trusting in riches can be found in renunciation of all you have.[9]

The rich man is cast in the role of an absentee landlord who has hired a steward to manage his estate. As a landowner he probably resided in a city, so he employed an estate manager who had full rights to manage the estate on his behalf, renting property, making loans and liquidating debts on his behalf. The fact that he heard rumours of mismanagement would indicate that he was an absent landlord, not present to judge performance for himself. We do not know who this rich man was.

Business was flourishing in Jesus' days. The factors contributing to economic prosperity were, good communication due to the spread of an international Greek language (Koine Greek, use by trades people and working folk), integration into the global Roman markets all over the Mediterranean, spread of the coinage system, some ambitious building projects in Palestine and proximity to important trade routes - to the east-west spice route and the north-south Kings highway bringing lots of imported goods.

Two economic factors influenced business in Jesus' times. In the Roman colony Judea, the economy was run directly by Rome using procurators and very large estates run by absentee landlords. These landlords divided the estates into smaller tenant farms upon whom a heavy tax burden was placed.

---

5   1 Timothy 6:17

6   James 1:10

7   Revelation 2:9; 3:17

8   Matthew 19:23

9   Luke 14:33

In the Galilee, Rome ruled through a very corrupt and cruel king Herod Antipas. Luke writes about Joanna, the wife of Chuza, Herod's steward or household manager, who was funding Jesus' ministry.[10] Smallholders on his estates would have had a very tough time under Herod and his wicked family and followers. The Herods were very greedy, considering the land as their own private property, confiscating land and expelling tenants. One farm near Shechem was over 2'500 acres and employing at least 175 families. Some aristocratic families also ran huge estates using small farmers to become rich. Such families often came from the religious elites like the Pharisees and Sadducees.

In Jesus' era, wealth and extensive property holdings were inevitable the result of corruption, manipulation and extortion.It would seem that this rich man was 'a lover of money' and the job of his steward who had to manage this situation was not an easy one at all. Although this parable is addressed to the disciples, the Pharisees, who were 'lovers of money' were listening in and ridiculed Jesus for telling this parable.[11] They probably identified themselves with the rich man quite easily!

One of the recurring mistakes we make, is about drawing conclusions far too quickly before all the facts are known. This was certainly the case with the 'rich man' who accused his steward of wasting his assets.

The Manager

The steward in our parable was an estate manager, a position of considerable authority and trust.

The steward was able to represent his master and act on his behalf, enter into contracts and, in general, attend to the legal matters assigned to him by his master. A steward could not be prosecuted for wrongdoing but could be shamed or dismissed from his position. As an estate manager, stewards were paid agents who also had other ways

---

10   Luke 8:3
11   Luke 16:14

to augment their income. Stewards belonged to the class of retainers who executed the will of the elites. A steward thus was one who was entrusted with the responsibility of the proper management of the belongings of another person or group and who was accountable to his owner.

It is clear that this steward was highly placed in the household administration of the rich and powerful elite. It is also apparent that the master relied on the steward to manage his estate and to realise a profit large enough to support his lifestyle and to provide the resources needed to fund his competition within the elite society he belonged to.

The steward therefore occupied a powerful, but at the same time vulnerable, position, since he was always susceptible to backstabbing from disgruntled debtors or tenants.

Our steward was a freed man and not a slave, although retainers in the household of an elite were nearly as dependent as a slave, but without the security associated with slavery. That he was not a slave is apparent from the fact that he was not threatened with being punished or sold, but just dismissed.

Christians often speak of man as a steward. The English word "steward" comes from the Anglo-Saxon words "stig" or "stye", meaning an enclosure or a hall, and the word "wéord," which means keeper.

In his book "Capitalism and Progress", Bob Goudzwaard presents stewardship as the norm of economic practice. "Stewardship consists of taking care of this world as the possession of the Other. It requires maintaining everything that bears fruit and being ready to give account for this." Central to this concept, therefore, was the maintenance of productive possessions on behalf of everyone involved.

In Luke's world, the Greek word *oikonomia* (the origin of our word economics) designated the behaviour of the steward whose task it was to manage the estate entrusted to him in such a way that it would continue to bear fruit and thus provide a living for everyone who lived and worked on it.

Accusations

So this rich man, owner of a sizeable farming enterprise, heard rumours of mismanagement and called his manager to give account of his management and accused him of wasting his possessions.

This word, "charged" or "accused" is the Greek word *'diablethe'*, which is the root of our word 'devil'. Our word devil is used to denote Satan, the devil who accuses us before God and the father of lies. This Greek word *'diablethe'* is related to the Greek 'diabolos', the accuser, or more often 'false accuser'.[12]

The Greek commentator Spiros Zhodiates in his book "How to Manage Money" says that the word *'diablethe'* is almost always used in the sense of 'wrong accusation', slander, and mudslinging. "This seems to say that the steward is being wrongly accused that he is being falsely accused of maladministration. Therefore, this parable concerns a steward who is falsely accused of mismanagement, or wrongdoing before his master. In fact, it can be argued that it is the master, who is unjust, not the servant."

Zhodiates says further, "the verb *'diablethe'* cannot mean anything good, and therefore it cannot refer to correct accusations. As the great Greek lexicographers, Liddell and Scott state that, *'diablethe'* means 'to set at variance, make a quarrel between, to slander with hostile intent, to deceive by false accounts.'

The rich man, then accepted a false or devilish accusation against his business manager.

Maybe this parable should, instead of the usual and most common title, 'The Parable of the Unjust Steward,' be called 'The Parable of the Unjust Employer!'

We are called upon to be good stewards and several other parables make this connection. So, I believe that the steward in this parable

---

12   2 Timothy 3:3 & Titus 2:3

is meant to represent us as believers and is designed to teach us how to respond to such devil-inspired, unjust accusations that may come our way.

Workplace gossip can be fleeting and harmless, but certain kinds of gossip can harm your reputation and your career. Employers must carefully and fully investigate any accusations of misconduct such as theft, harassment and discrimination, even if they believe the accusations are false. False accusations can have a lasting impact on your reputation. It is so important to base your judgement on facts and not hearsay!

If you are accused, make sure to get all the facts straight. As soon as your employer accuses you, start documenting what you know about the situation. If your employer disciplines or fires you, documentation will help you and your lawyer assess whether you have a legal cause of action against your employer. Write down everything you remember about any incident alleged to have taken place. Search your mail and calendar for any information that corroborates your recollection.

In the hierarchical economy of Roman times, working under a corrupt owner did not leave you with much choice. The manager did not, according to the story, fight back. He was accused of wasting the owner's possessions, but this could conceivably have been due to causes beyond his control. The harvest may well have been poor due to adverse weather conditions. The problems could also easily have occurred because of fraudulent actions from middlemen or tenants.

The nature of the accusation itself contains nothing criminal. The steward is accused of wasting his master's possessions. This very same Greek verb is used in the parable of the prodigal son, who wasted his own possessions. Our steward's management may have been unprofitable, maybe even negligent to some degree, but not dishonest.

Instead of thinking up an excuse, or making his case for good management, he decided to work out a clever way to make the best out of the situation, as a manager of a very unjust situation.

Stewardship

A manager of another person's assets should therefore follow the objectives and policies of the new owner. To this end, the owner will give access to everything he manages in order to achieve his objectives. "Here you have money, people, relationships, talents, open doors - use them to my credit, by serving people, by helping them to develop, by helping them to get to know my ways, so that my reputation is upheld."

A steward is a manager of someone else's assets. Only when we have assumed the status of steward and embrace the new goals, policies and business culture of the new owner will we find freedom in business and finance; freedom in bondage to Him who 'generously provides everything to us all'.

God is the Owner of all things. "Of the LORD is the earth and all that lives there, the world and everything in it."[13] "Yours, O Lord, is the greatness and the power and the glory and the victory and the majesty, for all that is in the heavens and in the earth is yours. Yours is the kingdom, O Lord, and you are exalted as head above all. Both riches and honour come from you, and you rule over all. In your hand are power and might, and in your hand it is to make great and to give strength to all."[14]I don't own anything ... everything that is under my control is delegated to me by God!

Richard Foster writes in his book "Money, sex and power," "We are imbued with the Roman and capitalist notion that personal property is a "natural right". The idea that something or someone could infringe our 'property rights' is diametrically opposed to our entire worldview. Add to this our seemingly innate selfishness, and it is clear why 'property rights' take precedence over 'human rights'."

The poet Shelley said, "Poetry is a mirror which makes beautiful that which is distorted." He went on to say that, "The principle of Self, of

---

13   Psalm 24:1
14   1 Chronicles 29:11,12

which money is the visible incarnation, is the god and the mammon of the world.[15]

The enemy of stewardship is not so much greed or possessiveness but fear; fear that the Lord is unable or unwilling to provide. You can escape the fear of losing something! Martin Luther said, "I have had many things in my hands and have lost everything; what I have put in the hands of God, that I still have!"

You can't lose what isn't yours! A shrewd and faithful steward knows this. When faced with loss, this principle will sustain you through very difficult times when things are being taken away from you. When the shrewd manager in our story was losing his job, this knowledge would enable him to confidently sit down, take stock of the situation and make plans for his future.

Did you transfer your business, job, career, finances to the Lord as the Owner, and accept the role of a steward? One of the most liberating decisions I have ever taken was to sign over all I hold to God and accept the assignment as a steward of all God returns to me. This will set you free!

Mammon would have us believe that we actually own and have title to the things we have in our possession. Mammon hooks us on to things and makes Gods gifts into 'mine.' In J.R.R. Tolkien's famous story of the Hobbit and his trilogy of the "Lord of the Rings," a ring is described, which is acquired 'by hook or by crook' and which gives the possessor unusual powers which could be used for good or evil; but they discover that the ring quickly attaches itself to the owner's greed and selfishness, corrupting them, eventually leading to their downfall. One of the characters, Gollum, is so corrupted that he called the ring "my Precious" and even turned against his friends to keep it.

That is exactly what our monkey, mammon, is out to do; to get such a hold over us, that we become possessed by our possessions and turn against people.

---

15   The Defence of Poetry. The Harvard Classics. 1909–14

THREE WISE MONKEYS

2

Luke 16:2 "And he called him and said to him, 'What is this that I hear about you? Turn in the account of your management, for you can no longer be manager.'"

The three wise monkeys

The lesson of the wooden sculpture of the Toshogu sanctuary, those famous three wise monkeys, inspires us still today. Its original message was simple and profound: "do not listen to what will lead you to do wrong", "do not see bad behaviour as natural" and "do not speak badly without reason". Interestingly, time and our Western worldview simplified the teaching a bit, leaving the classic "see no evil, hear no evil, speak no evil".

Our monkey, mammon, continually tempts us to neglect these wise principles. He wants us to do the exact opposite; to listen to what will lead us to do wrong, to see bad behaviour as normal and to speak badly of others without reason.

What emerges from the story of the three wise monkeys is first and foremost the need to always keep our spirit pure. It teaches us to avoid listening to anything that causes us to act badly. It says to avoid speaking without reason and to see evil actions as unnatural and wrong.

There is an interesting parallel between the legend of the three wise monkeys and this story from the Greek philosopher, Socrates who devised a "Triple Filter Test."

Here he talks about how a student of his came to his house one morning anxious to tell him a rumour. To the young man's dismay, the wise man explained that before revealing that news he had to think about these three things:

First, the rumour that you are going to tell me… has it been confirmed? Is it, in your opinion, a TRUTH?

Next, is what you want to tell me at least GOOD?

Finally, what are you going to tell me? Is it really useful or NECESSARY?

These three filters, as we see, have a lot to do with what each monkey of the Toshogu temple represents.

Note how in verse two, the master says only that he 'hears' this accusation, yet he has already passed judgement! Where was the evidence that this steward had done anything wrong? The master listened to the gossip and murmurings of others, but there is no evidence that he ever investigated the accusations against his servant! The manager was being asked to face some false charges of wasting money.

When the monkey, mammon, jumps on your back and pursues you, what do we have to do to get the monkey off our back?

First of all, investigate the matter. Base your opinion on facts. When you are accused, check whether there are maybe good reasons for a judgment of maladministration, or wrongdoing. If not, you can certainly defend yourself.

Paul was indicted to appear before the Roman governor Felix. He was charged by the Jewish leaders, saying; "We have found this man a plague, one who stirs up riots among all the Jews throughout the world and is a ringleader of the sect of the Nazarenes. He even tried to profane the temple."[1] Paul then defended his case because he knew he was not to blame for the allegations.

____

1   Acts 24:5,6

An important precept for Paul can be our example. "So I always take pains to have a clear conscience toward both God and man."[2] His conscience was clear and he could defend himself.

Paul remained in custody for two years and Felix was succeeded by Festus. Paul was heard again and said, "If, however, I am guilty of doing anything deserving death, I do not refuse to die. But if the charges brought against me by these Jews are not true, no one has the right to hand me over to them. I appeal to Caesar!"[3] He stood up for his rights!

Your conscience is a powerful tool in dealing with allegations. The word conscience, is from the Latin root 'con-science', meaning knowing together. The Holy Spirit reminds us of God's words and speaks to us, so we can know together what is right. If your conscience is pure, you can defend yourself, or admit you are in the wrong. When you ignore your conscience, you can't face up to it honestly and face up to your mistakes. The conscience is like a muscle. By actively listening to it, you can learn to discern between right and wrong![4]

It also seems that the 'rich man' has only listened to gossip, and spontaneously passed judgment without having bothered to uncover the facts. The Bible says that he only 'heard' that the manager was not doing a good job. Who is 'unjust'? We do not know that the rich man has investigated the matter properly. Where is the evidence that the manager has done something wrong?

Gossip is one of the most destructive phenomena for a company, church, club, family or other social partnership. It can destroy friendships, divide the congregation, damage or destroy good reputations, and stir up strife and envy. All wheat to grind on the mill for our monkey! The Bible teaches us: "A false character constantly sows discord, a slanderer drives friends apart."[5]

---

2   Acts 24:16
3   Acts 25:11
4   Hebrews 5:14
5   Proverbs 16:28

Accountability required

The manager had to get to grips with this and be accountable for his management. This is an inescapable aspect of stewardship. A steward is a manager of another person's property, and will regularly have to account for how that person's property has been used.

Each believer will once have to appear before the Judgement Seat of Christ to explain and show what he has done with the life and resources entrusted to him.[6] He will be judged on whether it was good or bad. The judgement of Christ therefore has to deal with believers who have to justify their lives to Christ. The court chair does not determine who was saved; this was determined by the sacrifice of Jesus in our place[7] and our faith in Him.[8] We should not see the Judgement Seat of Christ as a condemnation by God of our sins, but rather as an evaluation to determine the rewards from God for our lives.

The similarity of the talents in Matthew 25 illustrates the accountability three people had to give after receiving one, two and five talents respectively to do something with. One talent was about 6000 silver drachmas, and one drachma was an average daily wage. Quite a lot! For the two stewards who understood what they had to do and set to work, using the master's money, there was a nice reward. "Well done, good and faithful servant. You have been faithful over a little; I will set you over much. Enter into the joy of your master."[9] The reward for good stewardship was more stewardship! More responsibility, more to manage - and even more, the joy of his master! The one who had received one talent was scared and lazy, and despised the trust given to him by the master. He was severely sentenced.

I have asked many people what they would like to hear once they have come to our Lord Jesus Christ. I almost unanimously hear "well

---

6   2 Cor 5:10
7   1 John 2:2
8   John 3:16
9   Mat.25:21,23

done good and faithful servant". They want to know that Jesus is happy with the life they led and what they did with the means with which they have been trusted.

The Bible shows us in the parables of the kingdom that faithful stewards who faithfully use the resources of the Master, in His way, can expect that they will be partially rewarded in this life and in the next one, fully rewarded.

Honour and shame from the owner's perspective

Our parable is as much about the master's honour as it is about the character of the steward.

"Others" have told the master that the steward was wasting the owner's possessions. At this point, the story engages the social codes which have to do with the master's honour. He has in his employ someone whose actions cause him to be seen as a master who cannot control his house (οἶκος), and whose agent is either a fraud or an incompetent. The rich man looks like a fool in front of others. His social standing has been challenged.

Fundamental to the proper understanding of ancient Mediterranean society is an appreciation for the importance of honour and shame. The world of the New Testament is one in which honour ultimately counted more than wealth. To save face and recover a measure of his honour, the master resolves immediately to dismiss the steward, thereby acquitting himself of the charge of the inability to control his inferiors and recovers some of the loss of face.

The ancient Mediterranean society was an honour-shame culture in which the esteem from the public and especially of one's social peers is an intrinsic aspect of status. Much more is at stake in the parable than the master's money; his image and social standing have been challenged. Even though the steward belongs to the master's household, the matter of his alleged incompetence, or suggested dishonesty, has been made public. In one sense, it is not the steward who is on trial, but the master, and the court is the court of public opinion and of his peers.

In this situation, the master has only one real option, to dismiss the steward. The truth of the charges is immaterial since the master does not have access to a public court process in which such charges could be examined, and besides, such a process would only prolong the shame. Punishment of the offender is a secondary matter; recovery of honour is the central problem. His only course is to dismiss the steward and to do so quickly. Thereby the master acquits himself of the charges of the inability to control his subordinates and recovers some of the loss of face.

However, the steward's solution was a much better one, bringing honour to the rich man, correcting a dishonest situation and also securing new relationships for himself.

When you are faced with charges

The manager was losing his job. It is the privilege of a believer to be able to rejoice, pray and thank God constantly and rejoice in all circumstances.[10] When losing a job, or a major client, this is our invitation from God to look for 'the jewel in the mud!' Losing can cause financial hardship; it also presents emotional strain and stress. The anxiety and worry of being without work can also lead to a crisis of belief that can affect your spiritual health.

The great thing about signing over everything you think you own to God, is that if you do not own anything, you cannot lose anything! I have learned in life that the only constant is change! Money comes and goes, customers come and go, jobs come and go, people come and go. We have good times and bad times. I love what Job's life principle was. "The Lord gives, the Lord takes; blessed be the name of the Lord!"[11]

---

10   1 Thessalonians 5:17-19
11   Job 1:21

When change occurs, this gives us an opportunity to reset our calling and focus on Gods intentions in allowing us to fall into such a situation of loss. We know that, for believers, all things work together for good and God can take the waste products of life and make something better from them.[12] God is in the recycling business!

When things threaten to go wrong, mammon will jump on our backs and whisper into our ears that we are failures and accuse us of all sorts of things. Remember, our worth and identity must never be found in our job, social status or possessions, but only in Christ!

As Christians, we are so focussed on asking God for success, and almost think that this is a divine right. I am convinced and have experienced many times, that God can bless us just as much by taking things from us, as He can by giving things to us. I was brought up in a middle-class family, living in a nice home, my father had a well-paid job and we were quite well off. At the age of 16, I was in a fee-paying school, had quite a collection of postage stamps, football memorabilia, model trains and other stuff. My dad lost his job under puzzling circumstances and we had to vacate our home; our possessions were put into storage and we went to live with my aunt far away. I could only take with me what I could carry, and my dog! Later, all our possessions were sold off. I really believe that God used this to motivate me to search for the meaning in life, and soon after I became a Christian. I believe this formed my character for the better and made me much less dependent on material things for enjoyment in life, holding my stuff lightly in an open hand.

So, what new opportunities are arising from the new situation for the manager in our story? Well, he evaluated the situation, made plans and was praised for his shrewdness.

12	Genesis 50:20; Romans 8:28

THE MONKEY WRENCH

3

Luke 16:3 'The manager said to himself, 'What shall I do now? My master is taking away my job. I'm not strong enough to dig, and I'm ashamed to beg …"

The rich man threw a monkey wrench into the manager's plans!

The term, 'throwing a monkey wrench' is used when a project or plans are sabotaged. 'To throw a monkey wrench into the works' is basically the American English equivalent of the older British term "to throw a spanner in the works." ("Spanner" is the British word for wrench.)

The basic meaning is pretty straightforward, if you imagine working on industrial-age machinery with a big, heavy wrench or spanner. The 'works' refers to the machine, and if you dropped or threw a massive wrench into it, you could easily jam it up pretty badly.

Its history is apparently related to the "Luddites", a labour movement that sprang up in Britain in the early 1800s to protest the effect that industrialisation was having on living and working conditions. Protesters would "throw spanners into the works" to sabotage or damage industrial machinery.

Our monkey, mammon, uses monkey wrenches to mess up our plans. While God wants us to experience rest and peace, mammon is out to sow stress and fear and throw a spanner in our works!

What shall I do now?

Well, the manager's plans were well and truly wrecked by mammon's spanner! The rich man threw a huge monkey-wrench into his life, and this is exactly what mammon is out to do. He carries his monkey wrench and is constantly looking for ways to throw the spanner into the works of our life. This has been going on right from the beginning of work, after the fall due to sin. 'Thorns and thistles'[1] will grow up with our best efforts at work, seeking to reduce the fruitfulness of our labours.

Retainers and stewards could not be considered as an actual middle class since their power was 'derived' and the possibility of losing a good job and falling back 'into the peasantry' was a haunting companion. The manager wants to keep his same status, even after a possible failure in maintaining his position with the master. He was a free man and not a slave. A slave would have been punished; he at least got an opportunity to think and make some plans before giving his account.

When you find yourself in some trouble, it's always good to go away, look for a quiet spot, talk to yourself and reflect. Talking to yourself is sometimes not all that bad. The steward 'said to himself.' This looks rather like the Prodigal Son in the previous chapter of Luke who, after cashing in his inheritance and blowing it all on wild living, 'came to his senses' and started to make his plan to rectify the situation.[2]

Take time out to reflect, pray and meditate on what has happened and why.

"What shall I do now?" The manager had to start planning for his future after being fired.

---

1   Genesis 3:18
2   Luke 15:17-19

Honour and shame from the managers perspective

One of the 'social glues' of this pyramidal structure in that society, was the relational function of honour/shame values. Honour played—and still does—an important role in Middle-Eastern societies. The manager would have been well and truly shamed at losing his job.

Honour was universally regarded as the ultimate asset for human beings, and shame the ultimate deficit; so much so that Egyptian, Greek and Roman societies are referred to as simply as "honour-shame cultures". Much of life revolved around ensuring you and your family received public honour and avoided public shame. Shame is the feeling that you don't count, both internally in your own thinking and externally in your image in the physical world around you.

An ancient person would immediately understand the desperation of the steward's predicament here. He is being dismissed because he dishonoured his master.

A landowner was not supposed to shame members of the retainer class just as a retainer should uphold the honour of the landowner, and not act or speak in ways which would shame his patron. Maintaining his own honour and avoiding shame was foremost in the manager's thinking, while at the same time thinking of ways in which he would not have to put the rich man to shame. The balance was a delicate one, but one which had to be maintained in order to ensure honour was held high for all parties. He didn't want to be made a monkey of!

He was in real danger of being shamed, probably more important than anything else. He is forced into action in order to avoid social humiliation and economic ruin. With his dismissal imminent, the steward faced a major crisis. Being a steward was the only work he knew, but who would hire a steward who had disgraced his previous employer? The best way for the steward to either regain his position or find another similar position would be to somehow restore his master's honour. But how?

The steward chose to be vulnerable, and not go into defensive mode. Vulnerability is a powerful way of saying, 'you can see all of me, just as I am, in the situation I find myself in.' This negates shame and opens the door for solutions.

Vulnerability, allowing people to see who we really are, is a wonderful strength in relationships and opens opportunities for true communion with one another. Brené Brown, professor of psychology, has done some insightful work on this topic. I can highly recommend her TED talks about vulnerability. She says, "Vulnerability is about showing up and being seen. It's tough to do that when we're terrified about what people might see or think."

We sometimes associate vulnerability with weakness, fear, hurt or betrayal. These are the deep-seated emotions people experience when they reveal aspects of themselves to others. However, to be vulnerable is not a sign of weakness and can be your greatest strength. Brené Brown goes on to say, "Vulnerability is not winning or losing; it is not weakness; it's our greatest measure of courage!"

Mammon would keep us closed up, put a mask on and maintain that, to let people see who we really are is a sign of weakness. As believers, we can shout out, "When I am weak, then I am strong!" As Jesus told Paul, "My grace is sufficient for you, for my power is made perfect in weakness."[3]

Our manager chose to be vulnerable and was very honest with himself.

Crisis

The steward was highly placed in the household administration of the rich and powerful elite. It is also apparent that the master relied on the steward to manage his estate and to realise a profit large enough to support his lifestyle and to provide the resources needed to fund his competition with other elites. The steward

---

3   2 Corinthians 12:9,10

therefore occupied a powerful, but at the same time vulnerable, position, seeing that he was always susceptible to backstabbing from disgruntled debtors or tenants.

Our steward realised that he was in serious crisis and needed to do something to save himself. The envisaged alternatives were grim, meaning a demotion in the household hierarchy.

The steward's contemplation of his future position after he was dismissed from his stewardship comprised begging and digging, referring to common activities of day labourers. He could not even think of being degraded to almost slave status. He would certainly be condemned to a life of hardship and hunger. Losing his position would mean a kind of exile from the retainer class and having no access to any other household office.

Digging was the hardest work and was mostly done by the uneducated and the enslaved. For the steward to be dismissed from his stewardship, and to join the workforce as a labourer for day work, was to drop out of the retainer class into that of the expendables.

The steward had nothing left to offer but his physical energy, and, as a former steward, he would have little chance of competing for better work with peasants who had worked all their lives. The competition for work was fierce. Being used to regular meals, he would have to adapt to irregular meals interspersed with long periods of hunger. He would lose what little strength he had and would have become a beggar until, like Lazarus and thousands of others, he died from the complications of malnutrition and disease. His dismissal could almost be compared with a death sentence. If he lost his position, he would lose not just a stewardship, but his access to the household bureaucracy itself.

However, his fear of demotion in the form of hard labour and conspicuous dishonour lead to his desire to win the favour of his master's clients. The steward's impending exclusion is very real, and the image of being turned out is also closely related to the image of being cast out in other parables, such as that of the great banquet or the sheep and the goats.[4] There is also the correlative of being welcomed or received into the community of the blessed. We can recall the wise investors of the talents who were commanded to enter into the joy of their master.

The steward's words here do not necessarily mean that the steward is lazy or that he thinks he is too good to do the work of common peasants. Rather, they are a sober assessment of what he is and is not capable of doing. The focus of the steward's meditation is 'his position.' Since he is losing his position, he wonders what he will do in the future for employment. He feels that he must do something that will allow him to keep his position as a steward—either with his present master or with another—since he cannot do anything else. Something needed to happen, and quickly.

When in a crisis situation

When in a crisis situation it is good to stop what you are doing and contemplate the situation. Our steward, according to our case, only communicated with the usual 'un-holy trinity' of I, me and myself. What a privilege we have as believers to be able to discuss the situation, not only with ourselves, but more importantly with the real Holy Trinity! We can speak with the Father who loves us, with the Son who understands our humanity, and with the Spirit who will lead us into the truth!

Single situations do not define you, as mammon would lead us to believe. You are not each individual decision you make, but you are defined by the habitual ones, by the sum of all of them together. And when you feel your actions, or someone else's are starting to define something you never wanted to be, that's when you need to sit down with yourself and figure out who you want to be and start doing the things that will get you there and stop doing the things that won't.

---

4   Matthew 25:32-35

You can't plan for a life crisis. It arrives without warning, turning your well-ordered days into confusion and chaos. As you sit trying to make sense of what's happened, your new reality can paralyse you. Suddenly, even getting up from the couch is a challenge.

While there are many times in life when it's helpful to look at your three-year plan or reflect on the past during a time of crisis, it's much more helpful to zoom in rather than zoom out. You can't change what happened or know what will happen down the road, so focus your energy on right now, where you have some power, and work out what you need.

When you're going through a really rough patch, your first instinct might be to hole up and disconnect from the rest of the world. But it's important to remember that your friends and family are there to help. They are the ones who keep you grounded and focused on the present moment and help to determine what to do next.

You know, the journey of our lives is not just about the destinations we have reached. Our wisdom, education and personal growth come from the people we meet, the paths we choose to follow and the lessons we have learned along the way. We learn more from our mistakes, or tough times than we learn from good times. When in a crisis situation, it is our invitation from God to start praising and thanking Him for our situation. The Psalmist says, "The one who offers thanksgiving as his sacrifice glorifies me; to one who orders his way rightly I will show the salvation of God!"[5] When in a crisis, thanksgiving opens a door for God to work His wonders!

Interestingly, our manager realises his limitations and hits on a plan in which he does not have to depend on his own energy. This plan is opposite to what we would expect from a shrewd steward! The plan he makes focusses on his relationship with others and not on his own abilities. Instead of devising a cunning plan to squirm out of the situation, to lie about what had been going on, or to justify his handling of the problems, he decides to focus on others.

---

5   Psalm 50:23

He develops a brilliant solution: He intended to make his plans for building a relationship with others by trading material capital for relational debt.

IF YOU PAY PEANUTS...

If you pay peanuts, you get monkeys.

This saying means, that if you pay very low wages, you will only attract incompetent or unskilled workers (because better workers can go elsewhere to earn better wages). "Peanuts" is a slang term for low wages, and "monkeys" implies stupidity. If you want a top-flight design team, you have to raise your salary levels. If you pay peanuts, you get monkeys.

Our monkey, mammon, always uses money against humanity. Money is mammon's tool to tempt us to use people for financial gain. To get the best out of people, a manager needs to ensure that they are paid a fair wage, allow them to develop and not exploit them for financial gain.

The debtors in our parable were in a tough situation. Obviously, the rich man's business was not producing well in certain areas, of which we know insufficient detail from the parable. Harvests may have failed due to incompetence from the tenants or due to adverse weather conditions. The tenants under the steward's management were probably under a heavy debt burden and unable to pay as we shall see later in the story.

The manager was praised because of his shrewd decision to lighten the burden on the debtors, and for introducing them into a new reality of grace instead of subservience to money. Mammon and the power of money were being defeated.

Preparing for the future

In verse four, the original Greek word translated 'removed' is: '*methistemi*', from which we get our medical word metastasis. A patient goes to the doctor complaining about a lump, and after some tests the doctor comes back with the terrible words, 'it's cancer.' If things go from bad to worse, the doctor might inform the patient that the cancer has metastasised, meaning it has moved on to somewhere else in the body. So, our manager is being 'metastasised,' moved on and this gives an important hint at the meaning of our parable. The word is also used by Luke (a doctor…) to describe the removal of King Saul by God, to be replaced by David, which later brought about his death.[1] The word is also used by Paul to describe our salvation which was followed by becoming 'transferred to the kingdom of his beloved Son.'[2]

Our parable is all about this. Getting prepared for the future - a future in which we are about to be removed from this world to meet our Maker and give account for our lives. The parable is all about getting ready for future changes in our status. We will only live on this earth for a determined number of years and everyone will then be 'metastasised' into a new reality which lasts for eternity. Jesus wants us to get serious in preparing for eternity!

The manager's thoughts were, of course, short term. After his dismissal, he wanted to get a new job as a manager somewhere else, but Jesus uses this story to focus our attention on eternity. Preparing for the future is extremely important. If we don't prepare, the future becomes today so very quickly, with so little time left to do what's important! Winston Churchill is quoted as saying, "the better the perspective on the future, the better your decisions will be today."

---

1   Acts 13:22
2   Colossians 1:13

A pastor tells of when he was getting fuel for his car just before a holiday weekend. It was very busy, and he had a long wait. He went to pay, and the attendant said apologetically, "Sorry you had to wait such a long time. It seems like people wait until the last minute before getting ready for a long journey." "Yes, I know," replied the pastor, "I have the same problem in my profession, too!"

The manager is being removed from his position and has to find a suitable new position, and Jesus is showing us how he prepared for his transition, "Making friends for himself by means of unrighteous wealth, so that when it fails they may receive you into the eternal dwellings."[3]

Jesus speaks about storing up treasures in Heaven, not earth… something that requires an eternal perspective.[4] I think of our lives in terms of a dot and a line, signifying two phases. Our present life on earth is the dot. It begins. It ends. It's brief. However, from the dot, a line extends that goes on forever. That line is eternity, which Christians will spend in heaven. Right now, we're living in the dot. But what are we living for? The short-sighted person lives for the dot. The person with an eternal perspective lives for the line.

In the dot, we are consumed with the cares of this world: how big of a house we can mortgage, how nice a car we can drive, what the latest fashion trends in clothing are, and how big we can build our retirement account. In the line, we are preparing for an eternity with God and this is affecting our daily decisions, 'in the dot.'

Jesus told a story about a 'rich fool.'[5] It was a bumper year and when the rich man harvested his crops, his barns were overflowing. His answer was to tear his barns down and build bigger ones. Then he planned to retire and live the good life, to 'eat, drink and be merry!' There was clearly no consideration of who he could help with his unexpected blessings. He was looking to store it away to keep for himself as insurance for a life-pension.

3	Luke 16:9
4	Matthew 6:19-21
5	Luke 12:13-21

What he didn't know was that his life would end that very night. His focus was all about building treasure in the 'dot.' He thought little of the 'line' and as a result in God's eyes he was a fool. Living for the 'dot' is foolish because it is temporary. The wise, the shrewd, live for the 'line'!

Introducing grace

The manager could have used the little time he had left before his dismissal to say, "Alright, now I am going to lie or steal from my master. He is rich enough. Why should he have so much and I so little? I work hard. I deserve it. I'm going to get all that I can in the little time I have left."

He realised that this was not going to serve him well after his removal. He had a better idea. He asked himself, 'how can I make friends now, using my present influence, while I am a business manager, in order that these friends might help me when I am dismissed? I am still the business manager; how can I use my position to my advantage in order to get friends who will help me if I lose my job?'

Remember, one of mammon's sharpest tools is to persuade us that we must preoccupy ourselves with our own, present problems instead of showing concern for others. The time to show grace is when you need it the most yourself.

The evangelist Dwight Moody told of a stingy farmer who was recently converted, to whom a neighbour turned to for help. The farmer wanted to give thanks for his salvation by giving his neighbour a ham. On his way to get it the tempter, mammon, whispered to him, "give him the smallest ham you've got, you can't really afford this. You must be crazy!" The farmer replied, "if you don't keep quiet I will give him every ham in the smokehouse!"

The word translated "grace" in the New Testament comes from the Greek word '*charis*', which means 'favour, blessing, or kindness.' God's grace demonstrated toward man occurs most often in the Bible in the phrase 'favour in your (i.e., God's) sight', or 'favour in the eyes of the Lord.' This assumes the notion of God as a watchful master, with the one who is receiving favour, a servant or an employee.

Our manager showed favour to the debtors and acted shrewdly. Showing grace and favour will initiate a favourable reaction from the recipient.

Your customers are people – not businesses, shops, factories or schools. They need to be able to trust you. Trust is one of the most important aspects of doing business. It has everything to do with reputation and a good name. It takes long to build up trust, but it can be easily destroyed. Building rapport is a sympathetic connection to win their hearts. Many a deal has been granted solely on the basis that a buyer likes the salesman and wants to do business with him. With trust comes favour – the goodwill and approval without which we will never succeed in business! The principle of reciprocity means to give and take for each other's benefit; give and it will be given to you. It means granting favour first of all to the customer to build up a strong personal relationship. This brings grace into human relationships!

The Bible tells us of two very important qualities[6] we need to demonstrate in order to find favour with our clients. "Let not mercy and truth forsake you; Bind them around your neck; write them on the tablet of your heart, and so find favour and high esteem in the sight of God and man."

Our manager started to apply mercy and truth in his business dealings. In this way, he was currying favour so that the debtors may show favour to him. Wise advisors told Solomon's son[7], "If today you will be a servant to these people and serve them and give them a favourable answer, they will always be your servants." Kindness brings favour[8]. "The Lord bless you for showing this kindness to Saul your master by burying him. May the Lord now show you kindness

---

6   Proverbs 3:3,4
7   1 Kings 12:7
8   2 Sam 2:5,6)

and faithfulness, and I too will show you the same favour because you have done this."

The Principle of Reciprocity describes a human need for give and take in a relationship and by applying this principle, the manager was developing a new, healthy relationship with his tenants.

Received into a new economy

Jesus' parable is about introducing people into a new kingdom which has its own economy. Just as He said, "My kingdom is not of this world",[9] so is His economy not of this world. No surprises then that the solution the manager came up with as a 'shrewd' steward was nothing like what should be expected according to the world's standards.

The world economy runs by buying and selling, and in contrast the economy of the kingdom by giving and receiving. The world economy is a transactional economy determined by the laws of buying and selling. The economy of the Kingdom is covenantal, relational, determined by grace - entrance cannot be bought, it is freely given to those who want to receive Christ's offer.

Jesus allowed himself to become subject to the laws and power of the world's economy at the cross. He was bought by the Pharisees who paid hard cash (thirty silver pieces) and sold by Judas. At the cross of Christ, all the powers were present to celebrate his death. There was political power in the form of Pontius Pilate the Roman governor; military power in the form of Roman soldiers; religious power represented by the Pharisees; and the financial power of mammon, who used Judas to subject Jesus to the power of money. Thank God it turned out differently! Jesus allowed Himself to be subject to these powers once and for all, so that by His death and resurrection, all these powers could be defeated and that by this, we could enter into His victory!

---

9   John 18:36

So, mammon was also at the cross, subjecting Jesus to the world's economy of buying and selling. This mechanism of buying and selling is used by mammon to enslave people; money is his tool. The manager is being shown to be a shrewd manager in that he is introducing grace into a world of buying and selling and choosing good relationships over money.

Grace has been described using the acronym "Gods Riches At Christ's Expense.' Choosing to introduce grace into the marketplace is choosing to enter into God's economy, with all that can bring. It starts with siding with humanity against money. This is one aspect of the shrewdness of the manager as he surprised the rich man's debtors by introducing them into a new economy, giving them something they did not expect or even deserve. That's how God deals with us also!

John Wesley was a hugely influential preacher. While at Oxford, an incident changed his perspective on money. He had just finished paying for some pictures for his room when one of the chambermaids came to his door. It was a cold winter's day, and he noticed that she had nothing to protect her except a thin linen gown. He reached into his pocket to give her some money to buy a coat but found he had too little left. Immediately the thought struck him that the Lord was not pleased with the way he had spent his money. He asked himself, "Will thy Master say, 'Well done, good and faithful steward?' Thou hast adorned thy walls with the money which might have screened this poor creature from the cold! O justice! O mercy! - Are not these pictures the blood of this poor maid?"

Perhaps as a result of this incident, in 1731 Wesley began to limit his expenses so that he would have more money to give to the poor. He records that one year his income was 30 pounds and his living expenses 28 pounds, so he had 2 pounds to give away. The next year his income doubled, but he still managed to live on 28 pounds, so he had 32 pounds to give to the poor. In the third year, his income jumped to 90 pounds.

Instead of letting his expenses rise with his income, he kept them to 28 pounds and gave away 62 pounds. In the fourth year, he received

120 pounds. As before, his expenses were 28 pounds, so his giving rose to 92 pounds.

Wesley felt that the Christian should not merely tithe but give away all extra income once the family needs and creditors were taken care of. He believed that with increasing income, what should rise is not the Christian's standard of living but the standard of giving. His money management was to be characterised by the motto, "Earn all you can, save all you can, give all you can."

Mammon would say to us, "Get all you can, keep all you can, can it and sit on the can for as long as you can!"

# MONKEY BUSINESS

5

Monkey Business

In 1931 the Marx Brothers film called monkey business was released which was one of my all-time favourites. The Marx brothers were stowaways on a ship to America. On the ship they are forced to work for two gangsters and do the best to stay away from the ships crew. One gangster kidnapped the daughter of a rival gangster, and the heroes have to save her, using all sorts of funny tactics. The film is still hilarious!

As far as I know this is the first time that the two words monkey, and business were mentioned in combination with one another. After the Marx Brothers exploits, monkey business became a synonym for a kind of activity that is considered dodgy or questionable, but not criminal. Older brother, Groucho, a master of one-liners says, "Look at me. I worked myself up from nothing to a state of extreme poverty!" Zippo did agree that, "While money can't buy you happiness, it certainly lets you choose your own form of misery." Typical of our monkey!

The Urban Dictionary describes Monkey Business as: 'A word for any kind of shady activity, devilry, devilment, tomfoolery, dishonesty, trickery, chicanery, skulduggery, shenanigans, mischievous, devilish and deceitful behaviour.

Mammon is the master of monkey business. The goings on in our parable certainly look like Monkey Business! Is our steward being a cheeky monkey?

The loans

The debts mentioned in the parable represent the produce, respectively, of a large olive grove and of fields with an acreage twenty to twenty-five times that of an ordinary family farm. The characters in the parable are dealing with important commercial quantities and not just small household loans. Hence the borrowers seem to be more akin to traders or tenants in their own right, such as large farmers, than mere small sharecroppers.

It is not exactly known how large the quantities are, but anyway, these are very large. One commentator described one hundred measures (*baths*) of oil as representing about four thousand litres; and one hundred measures (*kors*) of wheat to have a similar volume of almost four thousand litres. The oil would have a value of around 1000 denarii and one hundred measures of wheat at a value of two and a half thousand denarii. The denarius was equal to an ordinary worker's daily wage, as Jesus illustrates in His Parable of the Labourers,[1] these days at an equivalent of more than $ 100.

In our parable, the manager forgives 50% of the oil debt and 25% of the wheat debt. In monetary terms, the relative discounts offered were roughly the same (the weights and measures are not exactly known); around the 500 denarii mark, which in today's money would be the equivalent of around $ 50'000 - a very large sum!

In the parable, it seems that the manager is cancelling only the interest related to the debts. That is 50% of the oil debt, which would be the interest on those goods according to known ancient sources on papyri, and 25% of the wheat debt. We know that is the interest which was levied on wheat debt as was later codified in rabbinical literature. In their book, 'Palestine in the Time of Jesus,' Hanson and Oakman state, "Rents of 25-33% of the grain yield and 50% of the fruit yield were not unusual[2]."

---

1   Matthew 20:1-16
2   Palestine in the Time of Jesus, K.C. Hanson & Douglass Oakman, p114

That this parable is talking about forgiveness of an interest burden is supported by archaeological evidence on Egyptian papyri of the practice of charging huge interest on agricultural loans.

Instead of a separate interest payment, the interest was often included in the principal sum, to avoid a sense of usury. It was quite common in the economy of the day to avoid interest on debts by increasing the principal owed. The early historian, Josephus, told the story of Herod Agrippa I when he was in dire need of money (c. AD 33-34.) He was given 17,500 Attic drachmae by a Near Eastern banker though the signed loan was for 20,000.

Restoring honour

The debtors in the parable were likely tenants or farmers who work the ground in their master's field and maintain his orchards. There were three categories of tenants – those who (a) paid a percentage of the crop in rent, (b) those who paid a fixed portion of the crop in rent and (c) those who paid a fixed rent in cash. The tenants in this parable appeared to be of the first type, since the steward could reduce the percentages they owed the landlord.

How could the audience hearing this parable think that by reducing part of the debts owed, this would help him to keep his position, or acquire a new position as a steward elsewhere?

As we have said before, the behaviour of the steward directly reflects on the employer or master. For better or worse, it is the master who is primarily judged by the dealings of his agent, not just the agent himself. This is precisely why the master wanted to dismiss the steward in the first place, because a manager's misappropriation of funds would reflect badly upon his master. Most commentators agree that whatever was loaned to the master's debtors was loaned at interest, and that the interest was probably exorbitant.

Horowitz in his work, 'Jewish Law,' says, "If an agent buys for less, or sells for more than the price specified by the principal, the extra profits belong to the principal not the agent." This does lead to an assumption that the principal, the rich man, knows the financial rates used by his agent. The manager was not giving away his own ill-gotten gains, but his master's.

The amount of the debt forgiven by the steward probably represented all or part of the interest charge, rather than the steward's own commission. Whether the steward is forgiving all or part of the interest, or even part of the principal we don't know; the main point is that the forgiveness of this debt will reflect well upon the master. The steward's actions make his master appear generous, charitable, and law-abiding. The debtors, and anyone in the community who hear about this, will presume that this act of charity was done at the request of the master, since the steward was carrying out his duties. This act would restore the master's honour in the eyes of the marketplace.

Forgiving debts

This parable is not merely an assessment of contemporary cultural values. Jesus' aim is to announce the Kingdom of God and the new ethics that it generates. Jesus employs the debt-remission practice as a symbol of socio-religious justice[3]: and debt-cancellation is taken as symbol of God's forgiveness and God's forgiveness as an appeal for debt-remittance.[4] The same root word is used.

If, as I believe, the steward represents believers, then our parable emphasises our responsibility to forgive. As God has forgiven us, so must we forgive others. Also, while we cannot even begin to repay our God for what He has done for us, we need to be about His work; returning what we can; making whatever contribution to the Kingdom we are able to achieve. The other side of the coin is also a valid interpretation. For the unsaved, the issue of forgiveness relates to God's undeserved forgiveness of their sin which is available through Jesus. The unsaved have a need, not only for this forgiveness,

---

3   Matthew 18:23-34
4   Matthew 6:9-12

but also to get their lives and accounts in order before they have to give an accounting to the Master.

The steward's act of debt-forgiveness is an act of beneficence to impoverished debtors. Although such an act could be reversed by the master, it cannot be done so without a severe loss of face. Instead, the steward has involved the master in an act of patronage, which would accrue both honour and a grace-debt to himself and the master. The shrewdness of his act turns on the fact that the master cannot reverse this beneficence without great loss of face, while the act itself has secured the steward's future; he is owed favour by those he has benefited!

The steward asks, "How much do you owe my master?" - indicating that the steward is cutting his master's profit and not his own. There is no warrant for the frequent assumption here that an agent could exact as much as 50 percent above a contract as his fee. The debt is clearly owed to the master.

The loans described in the parable do not seem to be under any kind of moral judgement; the matter of business loans is not dealt with specifically in the Torah. The steward is not diminishing debts on the basis of a religiously driven motive because business loans were not regulated by the Torah's laws on lending. The manager is shrewd, not pious.

Forgiving the interest rate on the loan or debt, is damaging to the master's economic interests. However, although the master is deprived of a consistent part of the goods to which he is entitled, he is also, from that moment on, depicted as a man of great generosity and therefore the object of great honour. At that point, he could only confirm and ratify the release.

The steward's future is assured by a reconfiguration of the socio-economical relationships between owner, steward, and debtors: debtors were released from the interest, while the master concedes the profit coming from accepted but still oppressive usury. Material goods of the master are sacrificed by the steward in the hope of assuring his own survival, a sacrifice that turns out to be a source of honour for the unwilling patron. If the master commended the wise, and maybe illiterate, steward, and ratified the new deal, he did so because he had no choice.

The debt reductions were not a falsification of the accounts, but rather a rectification of past wrongs. Rectification involves restitution. Restitution is a Biblical concept and has its origin in the teaching in Exodus chapter 22. We have a wonderful example of Zacchaeus who encountered Jesus and had a life changing experience. Jesus visits Zacchaeus's home, and the people who know the chief tax collector as a traitor and extortionist started to complain that Jesus would associate Himself with such a sinner. "And Zacchaeus stood and said to the Lord, "Behold, Lord, the half of my goods I give to the poor. And if I have defrauded anyone of anything, I restore it fourfold." And Jesus said to him, "Today salvation has come to this house, since he also is a son of Abraham. For the Son of Man came to seek and to save the lost."[5]

When someone becomes a Christian, he will have a desire born of deep conviction to do good, and that includes making restoration whenever possible. Restoration is a fruit of salvation.

This is a tremendous testimony and would reflect well on both the steward and the rich man.

When we make restitution after doing wrong it is also a very powerful testimony to our faith in Jesus and will bring honour to Jesus' name! Remember, Jesus' name, His reputation is what counts in the marketplace and we carry that name into the workplace.

Using money uneconomically

When we think of stewardship, we very quickly think of multiplying ability as we read from the similarity of the talents in Matthew 25, in which the Lord gave talents to three people, each 5, 3 and 1 according

---

5   Luke 19:8-10

to their ability. Productivity is praised when two of the manager's assets have doubled. The manager who hid his talent was severely criticised because of his default in carrying out the assignment. You could conclude from this that economic growth could be the only goal. There is a great danger of interpreting stewardship in this way.

Biblical stewardship is learning to use finance and ability for God's purposes and this means learning to use your money sometimes uneconomically! The mechanism of the world economy is buying and selling for mutual benefit and capital growth. The mechanism of the economy of the Kingdom of God is, giving and receiving, for mutual good and spiritual growth. Introducing grace often costs money and is in the eyes of the world foolishness.

Jesus warns us that we cannot serve two masters; we must choose between God and mammon. These two masters have established different systems of behaviour and economic principles and values. Jacques Ellul writes[6], "We can be very faithful to mammon by being conscious stewards of the goods and riches of the world, by making them multiply according to the law of money, by playing the economic or political game. Or, we can be faithful to God, having our homeland, not on earth but in Christ, seeking God's will, trying to live by his grace, but we must realise that this leads to an obvious ignorance of economic life in the world of money."

Jesus is asking us to penetrate the world of money with grace, being faithful to God as our only master.

Releasing debtors from their burden is an act of grace. A wonderful picture of grace is Victor Hugo's story Les Misérables." In this, Valjean, an ex-convict on parole, embittered by the discrimination he received everywhere he went because of his criminal status, had just been taken in for the night by a Bishop after being kicked out of everywhere else he had found to stay. In response to the mercy shown to him, however, Valjean robbed the Bishop's house and ran away with some silverware in the night. He was soon caught by the police,

---

6   Money and Power p96

to whom he then lied that the Bishop had made a present of the silver. Not believing him, the police brought him back to the Bishop's house to test the story, and secure Valjean's indictment. However, instead of taking his silver back and condemning Valjean, the Bishop tells the officers that he had indeed given the silver to Valjean, and not only that, he offered some additional candlesticks that Valjean had 'forgotten' in his haste to leave! In his zeal to redeem Valjean, not just in person but also in spirit, the Bishop had indeed turned the other cheek after being slapped in the face, and 'given his cloak when asked for his shirt.[7]' Valjean, unable to comprehend this radical act of grace shown to him, renounces his old life and follows the Bishop's command to 'use this precious silver to become an honest man.'

The Bishop drew near to Valjean, and said, "Jean Valjean, my brother, you no longer belong to evil, but to good. It is your soul that I buy from you; I withdraw it from black thoughts and the spirit of perdition, and I give it to God."

Valjean was redeemed by grace and entered into a new reality. That is the purpose of using money uneconomically; to introduce people into Gods world of grace. Is it possible to 'buy back' someone's soul through acts of selfless kindness? That is exactly what Jesus did for you and me.

Mammon would have us focus on maximising our financial resources instead of giving them away. When the goal of any activity is solely financial, we are serving the wrong Lord. The goal must first be service and then the fulfilment of financial needs will follow.

Remember, it is God who gives the ability to create wealth, but wealth for a purpose; to establish Gods relationship with Himself and also relationships between His children.[8]

The Archbishop of Canterbury, Justin Welby, says in his book 'Dethroning Mammon,' "The degree to which mammon is enthroned

---

7   -Matthew 5:39-40
8   --Deuteronomy 8:18

in each of our lives, or the culture of our society, is uncomfortably revealed by the degree to which we often disproportionally value the things we can readily measure."

We measure our nation's wealth by GDP, our personal wealth by "purchasing power" and most often our own worth in terms of the salary we earn, or the money we have saved. However, wealth, both corporately and personally, is starting to become valued by very different means these days, such as happiness, health, contentment, social inclusion and involvement.

Welby goes on to say, "Mammon draws our gaze away from things that are more worthy of our attention, but have not been given the badge of a comparable monetary value." A good example is the many hours selflessly donated in volunteer work, which is not given monetary value but contributes great social value. Perhaps we should, but that takes away the gracious nature of voluntary work. Welby says, "The beginning of dethroning mammon is to see clearly so that we may value properly."

We need to learn to value what is most important in life. Relationships in marriage and between friends, being generous with our time and money, physical and emotional health, inner strength of character, beauty and goodness.

The debts were huge and the discounts therefore also. I believe this gift of de reduction to reflect God's enormous generosity. Paul told the Corinthian Christians that God loves a 'cheerful giver.' This word 'cheerful' is in Greek '*hilaros*' which carries the meaning of happy abandonment. A state in which no cost is counted, or risk analysed, but in which the giver joyously shares with others with no restraints. That's the way God gives.

We are so conditioned by the economic notion of scarcity which the world's economy operate by. Economics, say the experts, is the distribution of scarce resources. Well, the economy of the Kingdom does not work that way. God does not know scarcity! Mammon sells us the lie that we cannot afford to be hilariously generous, because 'it is not good business', or we might need it in the future, or 'I cannot afford it.' This shows Gods ability to provide all we need, at all times, to do all He is asking us to do! Scarcity is a lie of mammon, deceiving us to keep hold of what we have.

Biblical stewardship is all about being willing to use our money uneconomically. A prime example of this is when Mary took a pound of extremely expensive, perfumed ointment and poured it over Jesus' feet. Judas, in charge of the disciple's money, exclaimed, "Why was this ointment not sold for three hundred denarii and given to the poor?" The account goes on to say that Judas was not really concerned about the poor at all. "He said this, not because he cared about the poor, but because he was a thief, and having charge of the moneybag he used to help himself to what was put into it."[9] This was an occurrence of mammon trying to disturb the anointing of Jesus, pointing to Jesus' sacrifice as our High Priest.

This act of worshipping Jesus by Mary had a value of one year's salary! Judas is saying what most people think. Mammon would cry out, 'Extravagant, uneconomic, what a waste!' If I am honest, this wondrous act of Mary's makes me uncomfortable … but I realise that worshipping God means yielding everything I have to Him in love, knowing that he is worth it. Then I can give hilariously!

Francis Bacon likened money to dung or manure. It stinks and is no use unless it be spread around!

---

9   John 12:3-6

WELL I'LL BE A MONKEY'S UNCLE

6

Luke 16:8 "The master commended the dishonest manager for his shrewdness. For the sons of this world are more shrewd in dealing with their own generation than the sons of light."

Well, I'll be a monkey's uncle

In the 19th century, Charles Darwin published two books, 'On the Origin of Species' (1859) and 'Decent of Man' (1871). In both of these books, Darwin shared his theory of evolution: that man evolved from apes, monkeys. Many people did not agree with Darwin's theories and the phrase "I'll be a monkey's uncle!" began to be used sarcastically by those opposed to the theory.

The saying is used to show grave doubts about any and all seemingly improbable situations. It can also be used to acknowledge the impossibility of a situation, in the same way that 'pigs might fly' is used.

This is surely a most improbable situation if our manager is praised for being what a lot of Bible commentators called 'dishonest!' How could this be? Well, it wasn't!

The manager of the monkey

Why the manager was praised for doing what many people and also many Bible translators and commentators think was a dishonest deed, is indeed puzzling. The key word translated 'dishonest' is in Greek, '*adikia*.' The phrase 'dishonest manager' is better translated as, 'manager of dishonesty.' The manager had to manage a dishonest situation which was imposed on him by a rich man seeking to increase his wealth to the cost of others.

Here we see a similar use of the description in the following verse 9 which we will discuss later. Jesus talks about 'unrighteous wealth', which is in Greek, 'the mammon of unrighteousness.'

It seems logical then, to equate the word '*adikia*' (unjust) in verse 8 with the money (mammon) which the steward was dealing with, rather than applying it to the steward himself. The servant is not unrighteous, in dealing with this 'unrighteous money' but I reckon his master, the rich man, is.

The manager, our steward, has a tough task! To manage something which does not want to be managed but wants to control. The only way to break this power is to choose God's grace and side with people against money. Money is a good servant, but a bad master and when we use money instead of allowing it to use us, and focus on God's will for our finances, we will be praised for being shrewd. In a marketplace which is under mammon influence and in a workplace in which mammon constantly tries to disrupt relationships, our assignment is to manage unrighteous situations which crop up at regular intervals. Managing the monkey who is tricky, devious and clever is a daily task in which payer and holding fast to Biblical principles is essential.

Our steward was doing a good job. By attempting to bring benefit to his master and restore his honour in his world, the steward is commended or praised by his master.

Shrewd

Our parable could have come directly from a collection of cases from Harvard Business School. A brilliant case in which the outcome is anything but obvious. One of the characteristics of the manager who came out of this situation well is 'cleverness.' Not exactly an aspect of the fruits of the spirit and not so directly connected with Christians.

The sentence 'the master praised the unjust steward' would make you think that it was Jesus who praised the steward and therefore approved the manipulation of the books and the loss of necessary income without permission. In this case, the parable is still referring to the 'rich man', the steward's employer. Jesus' comment begins with the second half of this verse when he noted that "after all, the children of this world are more intelligent with each other than the children of light.

The story was of course originally written in Greek, and the word we translate as 'smart' is *phronimos*, which means a well-considered use of *phren* or your thinking. *Phronimos* is the ability to rationally evaluate different alternative actions in view of the outcome. So first, think carefully before doing anything. The monkey is impetuous and impulsive and would have us work just that way. Being always comes before doing; what is inside always comes out, and that is what Jesus is talking about. Character first! The discipline of waiting, developing patience is a fruit of the Spirit.

When sending out seventy disciples on mission, the same word *phronimos* was used when Jesus said, "I am sending you out like sheep among wolves. Therefore, be as shrewd as snakes and as innocent as doves."[1] In the marketplace which is full of wolves and in which the maxim is valid - 'shoot first or get shot' - we have to be as *phronimos* as a snake! We have to be clever, careful, awake, ready and watchful; there are plenty snakes around in the marketplace. The cleverest, the sneakiest is, of course, mammon himself.

An opposite word to shrewd could be 'naive' or 'credulous.' Without having to distrust our colleagues or business partners completely, we need to be clear-sighted and try to discover the real intentions of the other and to evaluate any offers properly. This is a sign of maturity, as the writer of the Hebrews says in his letter, "… who by constant use have trained themselves to distinguish good from evil."[2]

---

1   Matthew 10:16
2   Hebrews 5:14

We may tend to think of shrewd people as those who take advantage of others, but in Proverbs it carries the idea of making the most of resources and circumstances. If we understand shrewdness as 'clever discerning awareness and hard-headed acumen,' then we see the kind of shrewd wisdom God intends for us.

A shrewd worker employs keen awareness and judgment. A manufacturer or craftsperson can have good judgement in selecting the right materials at the right price and quality. Investing in machinery, employees, or in research and development can bring good rewards in the future. A shrewd investor takes all risks into account and analyses the companies in which to invest.

A shrewd person is alert to all kind of problems which may occur and prepares contingencies. A shrewd person does not rely solely on his or her own insights but asks advice from others. A shrewd person constantly learns from their mistakes and improves their skills.

A shrewd money manager realises that managing money is not only a technical exercise of adding, multiplying, subtracting or calculating percentages. The shrewd money manager realises that managing money is a spiritual discipline, realising that there if a force behind money distracting us all the time from making good decisions as a disciple.

The French theologian, Teilhard de Chardin said, "We need to change our thinking. We are not human beings having a spiritual experience, but spiritual beings having a human experience." Managing money God's way, therefore, has to happen in the spiritual realm - following Jesus and rejecting mammon!

The whole parable of the "Shrewd Manager" in Luke 16 was told to teach us some crucial lessons about how to deal with money, and specifically about dealing with Mammon, the power behind money. Jesus wants to draw our attention with this apparent contradiction, to a businessman who was accused for acting dishonestly and being praised for it!He wants us to be smart when it comes to dealing with money. He dealt with a delicate situation shrewdly.

Sons of the world and sons of the light

"For the sons of the world are more shrewd in dealing with their own generation than the sons of light." We see two opposing expressions: 'sons of the world' (this present age; those who are devoted to the philosophies of this age) and 'sons of light' (those enlightened by the true light of God; our Lord Jesus, the Light of the world.)

The 'sons of this world' are unbelievers and the people of the world know that money is far from harmless: money is poison, money is power, and if it is used in the wrong way, it can destroy as few things can. But they also know that once you conquer money and learn how to use it, its power is virtually unlimited. Money has power out of all proportion to its purchasing power. Because the children of this world understand this, they can use money for their own selfish economic purposes. And use it they do! Money is used as a weapon to bully people and to keep them in line. Money is used to 'buy' prestige and honour. Money is used to enlist the allegiance of others. Money is used to corrupt people. Money is used for many things; it is one of the greatest powers in human society. We, sons of the light, are to use money in just the opposite way; to help people develop and flourish.

We are not to distance ourselves from the world. We live in it and can enjoy all the good things that God gives us. We are to use money but not let it use us.

We need to be 'sons of the light', learning from Jesus who is 'the Light of the world.' He said, "I am the light of the world. Whoever follows me will never walk in darkness but will have the light of life."[3] In managing money, we have to be guided by the Bible, which has so much to say about handling money and which principles and commands will 'lighten our path.'[4]

____

3   John 8:12
4   Psalm 119:105

Sons of the light will express the fruit of the Spirit in their management of money. Love (using money to improve the lives of others), joy (thanking God for all He has given us to enjoy), peace (quietly trusting Him for our provision), patience (waiting on God for His timing when making decisions), kindness (giving to those who are in need), goodness (being honest and true in our financial dealings, faithfulness (obeying Gods principles), gentleness (when dealing with others who are not meeting their obligations to you, self-control (in spending).

THE MONKEY AND THE JAR

7

Luke 16:9 "And I tell you, make friends for yourselves by means of unrighteous wealth, so that when it fails they may receive you into the eternal dwellings."

The story of the monkey and the jar tells of trappers, who found the best way to catch a monkey was, to take a jar with a narrow neck, put a fig inside, and then put the jar inside a cage. The monkey would come along, reach inside the cage, and put his hand into the jar to grab the fig. When he tried to pull his hand out he couldn't get it out unless he let go of the fig, which he would not do. He was trapped because the jar wouldn't fit through the bars!

And that's the same with us. If we hold on to our money with a closed fist, it traps us. It becomes our focus, our sense of identity, our worth. Only when we open our hands and loosen our grip will we become free. I constantly ask myself, 'are mine open or closed?'

In the third century, Cyprian, bishop of Carthage, wrote this description of the affluent:

"Their property held them in chains; chains which shackled their courage and choked their faith and hampered their judgment and throttled their souls. They think of themselves as owners, whereas it is they rather who are owned; enslaved as they are to their own property, they are not the masters of their money but its slaves."

As Cyprian noted, if we don't give, we're acting as if we really own our money. That's not the case. God owns it. What do we have that we were not given? The cattle on a thousand hills are God's, along with everything that moves in the fields[1] . The whole earth is the Lord's and all it contains is His.[2] David understood this clearly, "But who am I and who are my people that we should be able to offer as generously as this. For all things come from You, and from Your hand we have given You".[3]

Giving is a tangible way to acknowledge the ultimate ownership and provision of our sovereign God in our lives.

As we become free from money, God is free to bless us. If our hands are open, it's easier for Him to put something in them! This doesn't mean that if we give, we will always get money in return. The economy of the Kingdom works by giving and receiving, so when we give, we will receive back in some way or other. An old middle-eastern saying is 'the hand that washes others becomes clean itself.' Solomon wrote down a proverb which says something similar. "A generous person will prosper; whoever refreshes others will be refreshed."[4]

Making friends with false mammon

The beginning of 'being shrewd' in the marketplace begins with recognising what Jesus calls 'the false mammon'. As in the previous chapter, we spoke of the 'steward of injustice', Jesus has now started giving His lessons from the story and talks first about, "unrighteous wealth, which, in the original Greek is 'the mammon of unrighteousness.' So we have to make friends with the false mammon - the mammon of injustice (*adikia*) - and not give mammon a chance to disrupt relationships, as he wants to do, but rather strengthen relations and demonstrate justice in all our dealings.

---

1   Psalm 50:10-11
2   Psalm 24:1
3   I Chronicles 29:14
4   Proverbs 11:25

Jesus is explaining that money is not neutral but is controlled by a power which is inherently dishonest and will always, if not managed correctly, leads us into an unrighteous situation. He unmasked this power and called it 'mammon.' The old adage of Lord Acton remains true, "Power corrupts, and absolute power corrupts absolutely." Mammon has clearly defined his corporate mission - to command our service, adoration and obedience! His market positioning is to compete directly with God in order to squeeze God out of the Christian's life and work.

An ex-president of a very large bank is reported to have favoured his girlfriend by giving her a large, undeserved increase in salary. Since he was at the helm of the bank, this bank had repeatedly claimed that, 'The biggest obstacle to economic and social development is corruption.'

A promising leader fell by trying to make friends with money. I read in our local paper, "It was a beautiful career, which yesterday ended in a deep valley." This former HR director of a large car manufacturer and advisor to a German Chancellor, was convicted of years of bribery of the works council, including the payment of a brothel visit by staff representatives.

I think Jesus meant something else by asking us to make friends with money! These two incidents, which are constantly being repeated all over the world, are examples of how false mammon can be in our dealings with our colleagues at work. As always, it is Jesus' plan to work out His eternal goals, which have everything to do with our relationships. As an accomplice of the great seducer, the false mammon wants to disrupt rather than strengthen relationships. At first it seems maybe 'just a little thing', but as time goes on, such relationships that were 'created by the false mammon' come under pressure and eventually collapse. A definition of a distant friend is a friend to whom you have lent money! I remember watching a friend who had just lent someone some money. He gave him a big hug before they left one another. I asked, "why did you give him a hug?" "Well," he replied, "it's probably the last time I ever see him!"

Jesus wants us to make friends with the help of the false mammon with an eye to the future, and our eternal future. Jesus' life mission is recorded as; "for also the Son of Man did not come to be served, but to serve and give his life as ransom for many."[5] The ultimate goal is to spend whatever we have, so that our friends to be 'taken up into the eternal dwellings', so that they can enjoy eternity with God.

This reflects an important and essential ingredient of stewardship. Good stewardship is the ability to use some of your money for uneconomic purposes - for God's purposes to help people focus on God and on His eternal plans. In the first place by giving the 'first fruits of our income' and making sacrifices. Money given to the church, to evangelism, to widows and orphans and to the poor is placed outside the economic circuit. As we have emphasised, our global economy is determined by buying and selling. The economy of God's kingdom is determined by giving and receiving.

By giving money or forgiving debts, people come into contact with this other economy. An economy where grace, unearned favour, reigns. This also happened to the two debtors who owed the rich man money. They received something they neither expected nor earned. They could experience what it means to be forgiven.

I remember my first business outreach dinner. It was at an expensive restaurant near Schiphol airport, Amsterdam. The speaker was Bob Hage, a vice-president of aircraft manufacturer McDonnell-Douglas. Since my best customers were KLM and the Dutch Air Force, I wanted to hear him speak. However, I was only allowed to come if I took with me an acquaintance who did not yet know the Lord. I balked at the price of the meal - we could do our shopping for a week with the cost. Still, I paid for the lunch for a couple of friends. There, for the first time, they heard a testimony from a businessman whose life and work had been changed by Christ. One of them responded to the invitation to get to know Jesus. I call it 'making friends with the false mammon...' I hope to see him again in the eternal dwellings!

---

5   Mark 10:45

The emphasis on friendship is crucial. Jesus uses the same language here as in the intimacy of the upper room the night before his crucifixion when he said "There is no greater love than to give your life for your friends."[6] We are called to give up our lives, to renounce all that we possess, to use our ability to 'make friends' so that as many as respond may enjoy the fullness of eternal life with God. The material things that have been entrusted to us as stewards are primarily intended to be a blessing to others.

Jesus preceded us in 'making friends' with the financial entrepreneurs in the market. He was labelled 'friend of tax collectors'. He used all the material means at his disposal to show God's grace to mankind. The French professor of Sociology, the late Jacques Ellul, explains, "Grace must overcome the power of money, because when mammon is destroyed by grace, money is no longer a significant power."

Investing in relationships means entering into a kind of 'covenant relationship' instead of a transactional relationship. A "covenant relationship" is a relationship of grace, loving and giving something without consideration to others; and this reflects God's kingdom in which he invites all to a covenant relationship! A transactional relationship based is on 'you do something for me and I will do something for you'. There is nothing wrong with that, and we have to work in the world with such transactions, but this is a relationship based on market forces and subject to the influence of mammon, who uses human greed and dishonesty, to disrupt these relationships.

We read in the Bible that Jesus was furious in the Temple, made a whip, and shouted to the traders of sacrificial animals and the money changers. "Get these out of here! Stop turning my Father's house into a market!"[7] His anger came from the fact that trade and the exchange of money took place in the Court of the Gentiles. This was the place in the Temple where non-Jews were allowed to come to receive grace. Mammon was ruling where grace should reign. Mammon disrupted

---

6 John 15:13

7 John 2:16

the relationships between the people who had come to the feast to worship God. Mammon also disrupted transactional relations by offering sacrificial animals at exorbitant prices and poor quality, and by exchanging foreigners' money at unfair rates.

Access to God was obstructed by mammon, by the business practices of traders and money changers with the consent and cooperation of the Pharisees!

And this is precisely why Jesus tells us to 'make friends' by means of this 'unrighteous mammon.' Rather than running from money, we are to take it, use it and invest it for kingdom purposes! We are to be absolutely clear about the venomous nature of money. But rather than reject it we are to conquer it and use it for non-economic purposes. Money is to be captured, subdued, and used for greater goals. We are called to use money to advance the kingdom of God. What a tragedy it is if all we do is use money in the ordinary ways and not make any greater use of it.

Metastasised again

The phrase 'being received into eternal dwellings' was, according to Greek Lexicons, very common in ancient Greek. The term 'when it fails' uses the word '*methisteemi*' indicating 'to die, involving one's removal from life.' Greeks still use this word today (metastasis) to describe one's dearest being removed from one world to the next.

In the end, money will 'fail' ... there will come a time when money will no longer be available. It is well known that we are rushing into a world without cash. We are almost there! In the near future we will be in an economy with only electronic money - a marketplace in which, according to the Bible, it will be impossible to do business if we do not carry the 'brand of the beast'. Only people with that sign - that is to say, the name of the beast or the number of that name - could buy or sell anything.[8] Mammon will eventually be able to gain complete control of the market and complete his grip on the people.

---

8   Revelation 13:16,17

Fortunately, that is not the end of the story. Jesus will eventually triumph and take us to "the eternal tents" where he has prepared a special place for us! Mammon's influence will no longer be felt there. It is there that we desire to take people along with us and use our resources, our money, to bring as many people as possible to the eternal dwellings.

In our parable, Jesus is teaching us that we are all going to be 'metastasised' from this world in which we now live, into the next world which is waiting for us.

Making "friends" referred to patron-client relationships in the Greco-Roman world in which economic and social benefits were traded. This was seen simply as a social reality which could not be avoided (in the same way that purchasing goods with money cannot be avoided in our time).

The manager made "friends" in order to be repaid in social dividends whereas throughout Luke's Gospel Jesus teaches that making "friends" was to be done without hope of reciprocation. "Give to everyone who begs from you, and from one who takes away your goods do not demand them back.[9]" "But love your enemies, and do good, and lend, expecting nothing in return, and your reward will be great.[10] "

Jesus calls us to genuinely make friends with those who cannot repay us thus creating social unity between rich and poor.

It is these acts of compassion that have a bearing on our ultimate judgement – "make friends for yourselves by means of mammon, so that when it fails they may receive you into the eternal dwellings."

Using money for eternity

Our parable describes a kind of born-again stewardship - using what you have been entrusted exactly as the Master would wish, for His eternal goals!

---

9   Luke 6:30
10   Luke 6:35

"When the voice of the Master is calling
And the gates into heaven unfold
And the saints of all ages are gathering
and are thronging the city of gold
How my heart shall o'erflow with rapture
If a brother shall greet me and say
"You have pointed my footsteps to heaven,
You told me of Jesus the Way"

One question to ask is, "What will be in heaven?" Obviously, there will be people in heaven; thus one way we lay up treasure in heaven is to invest in the lives of people. That kind of investment we will indeed take with us. Money invested in people is the best possible investment.

Suppose that a country decided to change over its entire currency to dollars, and that the moment it did, all their previous currency would be worthless, but that we were not told when the monetary conversion would take place. In that situation, the wise course would be to turn our money into dollars, keeping only enough of our present currency to live day to day.

Now this gives us something of the picture Jesus means to convey when he tells us to lay up treasure in heaven and to make friends with unrighteous mammon. The proper use of money is not for living high down here; that would be a very poor investment indeed. No, the proper use of money is for investing as much of it as possible in the lives of people, so that we will have treasure in heaven. Of course, we need to keep a certain amount of money in order to carry on the day-to-day business of life, but we want to free up as much as we possibly can in order to place it where the return is eternal.

The children of light are faced with the great challenge of finding ways to convert 'filthy lucre' into kingdom enterprises. Money, evil tendency and all, is to be mastered and turned into kingdom opportunities. Perhaps there is a needy neighbour next door, or a famine in the Sudan, or an opportunity to spread the gospel to a hitherto unreached group of people, or a chance to invest in the future of a bright young student. These are all wonderful investment opportunities.

THE INVISIBLE MONKEY

8

Luke 16:10 "One who is faithful in a very little is also faithful in much, and one who is dishonest in a very little is also dishonest in much."

One of the big problems in managing money is that we fail to see the reality behind money. Money is not merely pieces of paper or metal coins, or bytes of information, but there is a spiritual power guiding, moving, directing and leading all of us using money. We do not see this reality!

Psychologists studied in 1999[1], a phenomenon called 'in-attentional blindness.' The so-called "Did You See The Gorilla" test had volunteers watching a video where two groups of people — some dressed in white, some in black — are passing basketballs around. The volunteers were asked to count the passes among players dressed in white while ignoring the passes of those in black. When asked if they saw the gorilla, most did not. More than half of watchers completely missed a person in a gorilla suit walking in and out of the scene thumping its chest!

Now research delving further into this effect shows that people who know that such a surprising event is likely to occur are no better at noticing other unforeseen events — and may even be worse at noticing them — than others who aren't expecting the unexpected.

---

1   https://youtu.be/vJG698U2Mvo

People can focus so hard on something, that they become blind to the unexpected, even when staring right at it! When one develops "in-attentional blindness," as this effect is called, it becomes easy to miss details when one is not looking out for them. Daniel Simons, one of the scientists who devised the experiment said, "Although people do still try to rationalise why they missed the gorilla, it's hard to explain such a failure of awareness without confronting the possibility that we are aware of far less of our world than we think."

We do not see our monkey - mammon - as he actively attempts to move us away from Gods standards in managing money. Jesus called mammon 'very little' and if we are not faithful in managing this 'very little' mammon (which goes unnoticed), we will fall into 'adikia' - unrighteousness.

An important tact of mammon is to remain unspoken of. Mammon surrounds himself with smoke and mirrors, so that we do not see him clearly. We have a kind of blind spot, so that we do not see his activity around us. "The god of this age has blinded the minds of unbelievers, so that they cannot see the light of the gospel that displays the glory of Christ, who is the image of God."[2]

Talking about money seems to be a taboo, even in our churches. It surprises me that we do not talk about money and possessions in church, even while money issues form a very large part of our lives. We talk about them every day, but do not teach a Biblical view in our churches! Just what mammon likes.

Faithfulness

With the story of the steward in Luke 16, Jesus wants to give us a perspective on the correct use of money. In verses 10-12, He gives us three word-pairs that help us to use money, without being used by it. The three word-pairs are:

'Little - much;' 'false - real' and 'another's - ours.'

---

2   2 Corinthians 4:4

With these contradictions Jesus wants to teach us to use money as our servant. Let us discuss the first pair. 'Little - much.'

Faithfulness in little things is the supreme standard to which a good steward should adhere to. It is a prerequisite to be trusted in much! Jesus told a faithful steward, being rewarded by his master, 'Well done, good and faithful servant! You have been faithful with a few things; I will put you in charge of many things. Come and share your master's happiness!'[3]

This emphasises learning to deal with the 'mammon of injustice' at the beginning of our responsibilities, when the resources we have to manage are relatively small. It is also important that business people who have larger budgets to manage are reliable in managing their private finances! If it doesn't work at home, you shouldn't export it!

Many times we are impressed by those who accomplish tremendous feats of faith in God. We are tempted to see them as great spiritual warriors when the reality is that they learned faithfulness in the small things first.

Moses, although being brought up as a prince of Egypt, had to tend sheep for forty years before being called into service to God. He had to learn faithfulness in small things. Joshua had to spend many years assisting Moses, before he could be trusted with the great leadership task of guiding Israel into the promised land. It was through Eliab, the eldest brother of David that we know that the flock which David was tendering in the bush was actually quite small. Eliab said, "… with whom did you leave those few sheep in the wilderness?"[4] And yet in his account to Saul, David risked his life for such a few sheep in the face of a lion and a bear.[5] This is God's mindset: If this boy could risk his life for a few sheep; he would no doubt take good care of many sheep. When the throne of Israel was vacant and God was looking for a faithful man to whom He could commit the nation of Israel, God's eyes located David.

---

3   Matthew 25:21
4   1 Samuel 17.28
5   1 Sam 17.34-36

Trust only comes from observing what people are doing with the tasks they have to accomplish with the resources they have to manage.

I was surprised with my first assignment given to me in my very first job after graduating in chemistry and business administration. As a fresh graduate, thinking that I knew it all, and expecting a responsible job in marketing industrial chemicals, I was assigned to assist an old, veteran salesman to assist in selling cleaning chemicals to garages and transport companies in London. My boss said, "you need to get your hands dirty demonstrating degreasers and learn how to deal with rough garage foremen." Not a dream job for a fresh, young academic! However, I was being tested to see if I faithfully carried out this assignment. After a tough year, I was brought back into the office to start a marketing services department, and another year later asked to start a subsidiary business in Holland. Trust has to be earned, starting with the small things.

We live in a world where faithfulness is a rare quality. To be faithful is to be loyal, steadfast, resolute truthful. It means to be firm in adherence to whatever you owe allegiance to. It is a characteristic of God and He expects us as His children to exhibit faithfulness in all our dealings because he created us in His image and likeness.

Mother Teresa said, "Be faithful in small things because it is in them that your strength lies."

Dishonesty

Jesus states that if I am unreliable in small things, I will not be reliable with much.

Mammon wants to lead us into dishonesty by claiming expenses that we have not incurred, by making how we offer our products or service see more attractive than they are, or by acting unfairly. God tests your reliability by dealing with money, especially in our tax returns, expense claims, and payment morality.

A very succinct and precise moral code was given to Moses. "Do not steal. Do not lie. Do not deceive one another."[6]

Whenever I take the time to meditate on this simple code, I get convicted and have to confess … I am constantly being tempted to break it!

When we think of stealing, we automatically think of stealing in a big way; but how about downloading software, music or films from illegal sites? How about stealing from the government by not declaring income?

When looking to employ someone, I always ask for references and always check them. It was astounding to discover how many candidates lied on their CV. I always test them on how faithful they are in carrying out a promise to send me something, or to be on time.

One of mammon's tricks is to say, "ah, everyone is doing it. It is generally accepted." This doesn't mean that it is right. God's standards are much higher than those of the world. It is so important to establish a sound basis for our financial management. If I allow a little dishonesty, the door is wide open for mammon to come in and perform his tricks!

Money as a test

God uses money as a test to measure my faithfulness and honesty. All of us have to make daily decisions about whether to handle money honestly. Do you tell the cashier at the shop when you receive too much change? Have you ever tried to sell something and been tempted not to tell the whole truth because you might lose the sale?

These decisions are more difficult when so many around us are, at best economical with the truth, or at worse, are dishonest. After pumping €30 worth of petrol in my car, I asked for a receipt. The

---

6   Leviticus 19:11

attendant offered me a receipt for €50. After pointing out that I only spent € 30, he replied, "Oh, that's for the accounts, you can claim the expense from your company and the company gets tax deduction. It's what everyone asks me to do."

When I heard that, my heart sank. The verse that came to mind was "every man did what was right in his own eyes."[7] People today do the same thing, formulating their own standards of honesty and then changing them when circumstances change.

Truthfulness is one of God's attributes. He is repeatedly identified as the God of truth. "I am… the truth".[8] Being faithful in little is being truthful at all times. In contrast to God's nature, mammon is carrying out the devil's orders; tempting us to dishonesty. "… not holding to the truth, for there is no truth in him. When he lies, he speaks his native language, for he is a liar and the father of lies."[9] The Lord wants us to conform to His honest character rather than to the dishonest nature of mammon.

I believe God is watching how we use our money. To the extent we are faithful in using the little we have, to that extent will He trust us with more!

Mammon is a little thing

Mammon is really only a little thing, although he would have us regard his enormous powers! Remember Jesus "And having disarmed the powers and authorities, he made a public spectacle of them, triumphing over them by the cross[10]." We must learn to use the unjust Mammon as a servant and not as a master!

Remember the wonderful film "The Wizard of Oz", with Judy Garland? A great storm carries away Dorothy, her dog Toto and the whole

---

7   Judges 17:6:
8   John 14:6
9   John 8:44
10   Colossians 2:15

house, from Kansas to the land behind the rainbow. There rules the great and terrible Wizard of Oz, and has bewitched the land from his castle for a long time.

Now, she is stuck in the Land of Oz. Glinda, The Good Witch of the North, advises Dorothy to go and see the Wizard of Oz, as he may know of a way to send her home. Along the way, Dorothy meets a colourful cast of characters, including The Scarecrow, The Tin Man and The Cowardly Lion.

The crew talk to the Wizard, who looks like a giant floating head and demonstrates his frightening power by flashing lights and loud thundering noises. However, Toto exposes that the floating head is just an illusion created by a middle-aged man, who is the "real" Wizard, hiding behind the curtain, pulling the strings. The pyrotechnics were all a show. Thanks to Toto, the wizard is unmasked, loses his scary powers and Dorothy can go home again.

The moral for us? Mammon is no big deal when we realise he is unmasked and has lost his power … the false wizard of mammon has been dethroned and God can take over!

STOP MONKEYING AROUND

Luke 16:11 "If then you have not been faithful in the unrighteous wealth, who will entrust to you the true riches?"

Stop monkeying around is a great saying which means 'to waste time or procrastinate by doing something unproductive or unhelpful; to fool around or spend time idly.' When talking about managing money, mammon would have us waste our lives chasing material things, thinking that these will bring us joy and meaning.

Mammon's ways of handling money will not lead us into discovering what Jesus called 'the true riches.' It is time to stop monkeying around and get down to what really matters in life - the true riches which can only be found in an intimate relationship with Jesus and all that brings with it! We are monkeying around with all this world has to offer, while ignoring the wonderful perspective of being offered the 'true riches' offered by God!

C.S. Lewis stated this beautifully. "If we consider the unblushing promises of reward and the staggering nature of the rewards promised in the Gospels, it would seem that Our Lord finds our desires not too strong, but too weak. We are half-hearted creatures, fooling about with drink and sex and ambition when infinite joy is offered us, like an ignorant child who wants to go on making mud pies in a slum because he cannot imagine what is meant by the offer of a holiday at the sea. We are far too easily pleased."

Let's not monkey around making mud pies and focus on our holiday at the seaside! Let's start living for the line and not the dot!

John Piper says, "The possession of money in this world is a test run for eternity." Can you pass the test of faithfulness with your money? Do you use it as a means of proving the worth of God and the joy you have in supporting His cause? Or does the way you use it prove that what you really enjoy is things, not God?

False - true

The second word-pair is false (*adikia*) - true. The unrighteous mammon gives us a false view of reality.

We need to be able to evaluate the promises made by mammon when using money and evaluate what money and mammon claim to be able to deliver.

I discovered a way of testing for the false promises after listening to a police inspector at Scotland Yard who was head of the fraud squad. He was asked, "How can you tell real money from counterfeit money? You must certainly spend a lot of time looking at all the false notes!" The inspector replied, "No, I don't study the false notes at all. I spend a lot of time looking at real ones. Then the false ones really stand out!" We need to spend lots of time studying God's ways of handling money and possessions and getting His perspective on true value. When we do that, we will develop the ability to spot counterfeit promises!

When in shops, large bank notes are often tested for authenticity. They subject the notes to UV light in order to spot counterfeit notes. That's what happens when we shine the light of God's Word on financial plans and transactions - the false aspects will start to stand out and be identified as wrong. When our financial values are tested by the Light of Gods Word, then the counterfeit, false works of mammon can easily be identified and dealt with!

The atheistic philosopher Friedrich Nietzsche foretold at the beginning of the 20th century that we would replace God with money and that money would become a counterfeit god.

"What induces one man to use false weights, another to set his house on fire after having insured it for more than its value, while three-fourths of our upper classes indulge in legalised fraud . . . what gives rise to all this? It is not real want, for their existence is by no means precarious . . . but they are urged on, day and night, by a terrible impatience at seeing their wealth pile up so slowly, and by an equally terrible longing and love for these heaps of gold. What once was done for the love of God is now done for the love of money, i.e., for the love of that which at present affords us the highest feeling of power and a good conscience."

This was underscored by the Jesuit author and philosopher Thomas Merton, who said that "Mammon has demonically usurped the role in modern society which the Holy Spirit is to have in the Church." That role is, of course, to guide, to lead, to empower, to comfort. Mammon is indeed having this same role today; and I would go as far as to say that mammon is also replacing the work of the Holy Spirit in our Christian life as we neglect to teach a Biblical view of money.

Unrighteous wealth

Bible translators, in attempting to reflect the original Greek of this verse in such a way that is understandable to us, translated the original Greek 'mammon of *adikia*' (unrighteousness or iniquity)' into 'unrighteous wealth' or sometimes 'worldly wealth.' This fails to correctly portray the way money works. If not managed and used wisely, it always leads us into unrighteousness and injustice.

This unrighteousness can express itself in many ways. One of the most succinct descriptions is in Jesus parable of the sower in which he explains why the Bible can be so irrelevant to some people. One group of people in which Gods word is rendered ineffective is described as; "Others, like seed sown among thorns, hear the word;

but the worries of this life, the deceitfulness of wealth and the desires for other things come in and choke the word, making it unfruitful."[1] The 'mammon of *adikia*' wants to develop three life attitudes which would choke God's word; worry, deceit and desire.

We spend so much time worrying about money. How to make it, conserve it, multiply it and spend it. Worry is not productive and occupies our minds so that we often cannot think straight. Financial stress can cause mental and emotional problems, cause marriage breakdown and damage relationships. God wants to set us free from anxiety and experience peace and freedom, so that we can learn to be content in any circumstances.[2]

Wealth or riches are deceitful at the core because they make promises they can't keep. Money promotes itself as the answer to our problems, as a barometer of God's blessing and his ability to provide for us. It makes us think our value lies in how much we are able to accumulate, and it promises to provide a type of comfort and rest and abundant pleasure that can only be found in the presence of the Lord.

While I have never experienced true poverty, my wife and I have gone through periods of financial strain. We had some very tight years, following a career change and starting work for a Christian non-profit. I felt the Lord taught me a lot about the inclination of my heart to believe in the lies prompted by material prosperity during the lean years. I was surprised, however, by how much I needed to actively guard my thinking with biblical truth in times of want, just as much as in times of plenty.

The 'desire for other things' can really choke us and diminish the effect of the Bible in our lives! This word is a strong word and means 'craving' or 'lusting' after stuff. It is a consuming desire which puts all other desires to one side. Ultimately this leads to greed which is very destructive. "Stuffocation' is a new word which we could easily add to our dictionary. The trend watcher James Wallmann coined the

---

1   Mark 4:18.19
2   Philippians 4:11,13

term to describe the feeling that too many things, too much stuff is suffocating our way of life.

Thanks to mass production and global markets, we have access to a huge amount of relatively cheap products which we readily buy … and then store! The explosion of self-storage facilities over the past 10 years testify to the fact that we have too much stuff and too little space to keep it. Not only too little physical space but also too little emotional space. The excess of things is beginning to show us that more is, in fact, less.

That the cultivation of needs leads to unrest and dissatisfaction was also noted by the Dominican Friar Anselm Grün, who leads a very large group of businesses in southern Germany. In his book "Of Greek and Desire," he notes, "The attitude of never having enough leads to a nomadic behaviour and continual dissatisfaction. The desire for possessions is really a desire for rest. But the paradox is that we never find rest because we are possessed by the desire for more."

Idols

I read a great book by John White with the title "Money isn't God" and a sub-title of 'So Why is the Church Worshipping It?' I would add, 'so why are we all worshipping it?' The 'unrighteousness' of wealth lies in the fact that possessions can easily become idols. Idolatry can easily seem like a distant, abstract reality – something that takes place in Hollywood or Wall Street or Washington, or in the ads and shows we see on our televisions, tablets, and phones.

The great reformer, John Calvin stated, "From this we may gather that man's nature, so to speak, is a perpetual factory of idols. So it goes. Man's mind, full as it is of pride and boldness, dares to imagine a god according to its own capacity; as it sluggishly plods, indeed is overwhelmed with the crassest ignorance, it conceives an unreality and an empty appearance as God." This is exactly mammon's tactic - to lead us to believe that anything we can buy will fulfil desires and longings that only God can fulfil.

Tim Keller points out in his book "Counterfeit Gods", that the main characteristics of idols are when:

- Anything we make or buy is more important than God.

- Anything that absorbs our hearts and minds is greater than God.

- Anything that we seek, is to give us what only God can give (meaning, value, significance, security, etc.).

- Anything is so central and essential to life that if we lose it, life no longer feels worth living.

There is an insightful passage in the Bible which talks of the deceitfulness of mammon's promises. Mammon uses money to make promises which will not be fulfilled. "The idols of the nations are silver and gold, the work of human hands. They have mouths, but do not speak; they have eyes, but do not see; they have ears, but do not hear, or is there any breath in their mouths."[3] The promises look good, but have no substance and will not work out. He is out to create a 'virtual reality' in which he makes many promises which will never be fulfilled.

We think that money will bring us what we desire most in life, but the old adage is so true that 'the best things in life are free.' Indeed, you can buy a house, but that does not necessarily provide a home, you can buy medicine, but that is no guarantee of health; you can buy books but not wisdom; entertainment but not joy; sex but not love. We all tend to trust in money for what we need and do anything we can to get it, multiply it and use it to buy fulfilment and meaning. The opposite is often true. The more possessions, the more money, care and attention needed to maintain them; the more investments, the more care and worry needed to secure them.

The psalmist goes on to say that, "Those who make them become like them, so do all who trust in them."[4] We become what we worship!

---

3   Psalm 135:15-17
4   Psalm 135:18

Worship and serve the Lord, we find life. The atheistic philosopher, Albert Camus stated, "Any life directed toward money is death."

The Czech professor Dr. Tomáš Sedláček in his book "The Economics of Good and Evil" stated, "The more we have, the more we want. Why? Perhaps we thought (and this sounds truly intuitive) that the more we have, the less we will need. We thought that consumption leads to saturation of our needs. But the opposite has proven to be true. The more we have, the more additional things we need. Every new satisfied want will beget a new one and will leave us wanting. For consumption is like a drug."

Benjamin Franklin said, "Money never made a man happy yet, nor will it. There is nothing in its nature to produce happiness. The more a man has, the more he wants. Instead of its filling a vacuum, it makes one. If it satisfies one want, it doubles and triples that want another way."

Mammon's trick is to keep us dissatisfied by our constant longing for more.

Probably the richest man who ever lived up to our common times was King Solomon. He wrote of his striving for more. "I said to myself, 'Come now, I will test you with pleasure to find out what is good.' But that also proved to be meaningless. And what does pleasure accomplish? I tried cheering myself with wine and embracing folly —my mind still guiding me with wisdom. I wanted to see what was good for people to do under the heavens during the few days of their lives.

I undertook great projects: I built houses for myself and planted vineyards. I made gardens and parks and planted all kinds of fruit trees in them. I made reservoirs to water groves of flourishing trees. I bought male and female slaves and had other slaves who were born in my house. I also owned more herds and flocks than anyone in Jerusalem before me. I amassed silver and gold for myself, and the treasure of kings and provinces. I acquired male and female singers, and a harem as well—the delights of a man's heart. I became greater by far than anyone in Jerusalem before me. In all this my wisdom stayed with me. I denied myself nothing my eyes desired; I refused my heart no pleasure. My heart took delight in all my labour, and this was the reward for all my toil.

Yet when I surveyed all that my hands had done and what I had toiled to achieve, everything was meaningless, a chasing after the wind; nothing was gained under the sun.[5]"

In his book, 'Rethinking Materialism,' Miroslav Volf, the Croatian theologian, wrote these penetrating words. "If we eliminated all the contrived wants generated by either helpful or greedy producers, the squirrel cage would no doubt turn at a much slower pace, but it would not come to a halt. Consumerism is a creation of capitalism. Insatiability is not; capitalism only capitalises on it. The rootedness of insatiability in human nature leads to a very simple but fundamental insight: the economic problem cannot be solved by economic means alone, not even in a hundred years. The only proper 'object' of human insatiability is the mystery of the infinite God. In God, in whom nothing worth preserving is lost, everything worth enjoying can be enjoyed."

True riches?

Jesus also marks out a quality which distinguishes the truly shrewd operator from others, understanding what 'true riches' really are. It is easy to be completely blinded by the sheer size of mammon's rewards. We can come to the place where we actually believe that, 'treasures on earth' in abundance constitute true riches and create true happiness. The evidence points, if anything, to the precise opposite - the wealthier people become, the less contented and satisfied they become. Mammon promises so much and delivers so little.

But Jesus actually speaks more pointedly than that, because he stresses that access to 'the true riches' depends on the way we handle what

---

5   Ecclesiastes 2:1-11

comes from 'the mammon of unrighteousness'. If we cannot be trusted to handle these things with a proper shrewdness, notably in the way we use it to make friends, we are in jeopardy of missing out on the true riches of God's kingdom.[6] What Paul calls 'the unsearchable riches of Christ' will pass us by - in this life and the next.

These 'treasures in heaven' include such unparalleled wealth as the peace of Christ, the joy of the Lord, the forgiveness of our sins, the power of God, the presence of God, the gift of his Spirit - and much else besides.

I still remember a time about 30 years ago, when I was sharing my experience of these 'true riches' with a very successful young businessman. He listened and questioned me for a couple of hours. He then stood up, shook my hand and said: 'You're a very wealthy man'. To know God's grace in our lives is 'the true riches'. A shrewd person looks at mammon's treasures through that prism.

Renunciation

The antidote to the deceitfulness of riches, and unrighteous wealth is a simple word, but one which is so difficult to practice. That is renunciation. To renounce means to give up all claim to all we possess and hand all over to Gods direction. Jesus stated that renunciation is a prerequisite to be a disciple. "So therefore, any one of you who does not renounce all that he has cannot be my disciple."[7]

It was the solution to the problem of the rich, young ruler who confronted Jesus asking about inheriting eternal life. The answer was not obedience to the commandments but to 'sell all that you have and distribute to the poor, and you will have treasure in heaven; and come, follow me.."[8] Luke says that the young man went away sad, because he was very rich.

---

6   Ephesians 3: 8
7   Luke 14:33.
8   Luke 18:22

A basic requirement of discipleship is to live daily with a 'cross experience.' Jesus said, "Whoever wants to be my disciple must deny themselves and take up their cross daily and follow me."[9] In managing money and planning our financial life, we need to live daily with our 'cross experience.' Firstly, to realise that Jesus has defeated mammon's power at His cross once and for all. Then, to appropriate this victory daily as we deny ourselves mammon's promises and look to Gods leadership and guidance in our financial planning and decision-making.

Charles Finney, a pivotal figure in American evangelism was radical in this. In his 'Lectures on Revival,' he wrote in 1825, "Young converts should be taught that they have renounced the ownership of all their possessions and of themselves, or if they have not done this they are not Christians. They should not be left to think that anything is their own, their time, property, influence, faculties, bodies or souls. 'You are not your own; all belongs to God' and when they submitted to God they made a free surrender of all to him, to be ruled and disposed of at his pleasure. They have no right to spend one hour as if their time is their own. No right to go anywhere, or do anything, for themselves, but should hold all at the disposal of God, and employ all for the glory of God. If they do not, they ought not to call themselves Christians, for the very idea of being a Christian is to renounce self and become entirely consecrated to God. A man has no more right to withhold any thing from God, than he has to rob or steal. If God calls on them to employ anything they have, their money, or their time, or to give their children, or to dedicate themselves in advancing his kingdom, and they refuse, because they want to use them in their own way, or prefer to do something else, it is vastly more blameable than for a clerk or an agent to go and embezzle the money that is entrusted him by his employer, and spend it for his family, or lay it out in bank stock or in speculation for himself."

Wow, I wish this kind of radical discipleship was preached today!

---

9   Luke 9:23

When I was 30, my life hit a crisis. Up until then, I had vigorously pursued my view of success. A nice home for the family, high income, CEO of a chemical company. I was achieving all those, but I realised at that time success came at a high price. It was like I was standing on a ladder, leaning against the wall of success, and then looking around at the view from the top, only to discover that my ladder was leaning against the wrong wall. I lost my balance and came falling down. The price for success came in three packages. Firstly, my health deteriorated due to the stress of business and working too hard. I was hospitalised for some time with a stress-related hernia. Then, my relationship with my wife and children was suffering due to my long absences from home and lack of attention. Thirdly, my relationship with God was almost gone. I remember sitting in church one morning and the only thing I could think about was business the next day. Jesus' words came home to me like an arrow to the heart. "For whoever wants to save their life will lose it, but whoever loses their life for me will save it. What good is it for someone to gain the whole world, and yet lose or forfeit their very self."[10] I was losing myself - my soul. After that, I left my CEO job with this company and took a quieter management role in another company, so I could spend more time at home.

That which Jesus called 'true riches' can only be obtained when we completely distance ourselves from mammon's misleading promises, when we are ready to deny ourselves and no longer look to money and possessions to deliver what we truly need for a healthy, meaningful life together with Jesus, and building up for ourselves treasures in heaven.

---

10   Luke 9:23-25

THE CLEVER MONKEY   10

Luke 16:12 "And if you have not been faithful in that which is another's, who will give you that which is your own?"

Clever monkey

The Clever Monkey is a classic folktale from West Africa. One day, two greedy jungle cats discover a large piece of cheese. They want to share the piece of cheese but cannot decide how they can divide it fairly. A very clever little monkey loves cheese as well and when he sees the two cats arguing over the cheese, he uses this opportunity to divert their attention and to trick the jungle cats into allowing him to eat practically all of the cheese. Unfortunately for the two cats, they never realise that they were completely tricked by a very clever monkey.

This timeless folktale shares valuable life lessons in character values about sharing by overcoming greed, being resourceful, and learning how to judge who is trustworthy and who isn't. The jungle cats simply allow their greed to get in the way of sharing. They are more concerned about getting the biggest piece of cheese and their lack of trust enables the monkey to trick them into foolish decisions. Their greed ends up leaving them with much less than what they started with, because a very clever monkey used their greed against them and by the end of the story, he is the one who has the last laugh.

One of the ways in which our monkey, mammon, tricks people, is to use our inbuilt selfishness and greed. I believe the rich man in our story showed his greed by imposing a huge burden of debt on his tenants and making his manager enforce this policy of maximising profits at the expense of the tenants. Mammon ends up with the whole cheese.

Belongs to another

The third word-pair Jesus gives us is just as radical! He talks about what 'belongs to another' and 'what belongs to you'. We are raised to think that we are the owners of everything we have worked and earned for. The business belongs to me, my house, my car, my money. Jesus says, "No, it belongs to another." All my material possessions belong to another; in fact, an Other with a capital letter - God Himself!

In fact, we own nothing, we only have it to manage and utilise. The Bible is consistent in the doctrine that everything belongs to God. Whether it be gold or silver[1] the cattle on a thousand hills,[2] everything belongs to Him![3] Recognising that God is the Owner of all things, that you are just a manager of God's resources, is liberating and paves the way for us to receive what really belongs to us - the indwelling of the fullness of God with all that he wants to do in and through us and for us! Being shrewd is to acknowledge that I am the manager of what God entrusts me with, because it opens the way to the 'true wealth' that I can appropriate in the Kingdom of God.

The Bible asks, "Do you not know that your body is a temple of the Holy Spirit, who lives in you and who you have received from God, and do you not know that you are not your own? You have been bought and paid for, so honour God with your body.[4] That we have been bought and therefore should pursue God's goals naturally

---

1   Haggai 2:8
2   Psalm 50:10
3   1 Chronicle 29:11
4   1 Cor 6:19,20

applies to everything we have and think we possess - possessions, wealth, stocks, talents, gifts, experience, position, status, family, career etc.

Only when we have assumed the status of steward and embrace the new goals, policies and business culture of the new owner will we find freedom in business and finance; freedom in bondage to Him who 'generously provides everything to us all'.

To this end, the owner will give access to everything he manages in order to achieve his objectives. He is saying to you and I, "Here you have money, people, relationships, talents, open doors - use them to my credit, for my purposes, by serving people, by helping them to develop to their full potential, by helping them to get to know me and all I can give them."

The enemy of stewardship is not so much greed or possessiveness but fear; fear that the Lord is unable or unwilling to provide. You can escape this fear of losing something. After all, you can't lose what isn't yours! Did you transfer your business, job, career, finances to the Lord? That is truly an act of liberation!

Faithful to that which belongs to another

I just got my tax return assessment back from the tax office. Fortunately, I get a small amount back which was overpaid last year. Who likes to have to pay tax? Well, I do!

Jesus gave a brilliant answer to some religious leaders who tried to trap him with a question about paying taxes to the Roman government of occupation.

"Is it lawful to pay taxes to Caesar, or not? Should we pay them, or should we not?" But, knowing their hypocrisy, he said to them, "Why put me to the test? Bring me a denarius and let me look at it." And they brought one. And he said to them, "Whose likeness and inscription is this?" They said to him, "Caesar's." Jesus said to them,

"Render to Caesar the things that are Caesar's, and to God the things that are God's." And they marvelled at him."[5]

What is God's? The answer: Everything is God's. So the point seems to be: When you realise that all of life, including all of Caesar's rights and power and possessions belong to God, then you will be in a proper frame of mind to render to Caesar what is Caesar's. When you know that all is God's, then anything you render to Caesar you will render for God's sake. Any authority you ascribe to Caesar you will ascribe to him for the sake of God's greater authority. Any obedience you render to Caesar you will render for the sake of the obedience you owe first to God. Any claim Caesar makes on you, you test by the infinitely higher claim God has on you.

What is Caesar's is determined by the fact that everything is God's first, and only becomes Caesar's by God's permission and design. Only God decides what is a rightful, limited rendering to Caesar. The only reason God ordains the rights of a Caesar is for the sake of God.

Therefore, Peter could say, "Be subject for the Lord's sake to every human institution, whether it be to the emperor as supreme or to governors as sent by him"[6]

Jesus and Peter are calling for Christians to have the mindset of an alien and an citizen at the same time. "Live as free people, not using your freedom as a cloak of evil, but being servants of God."[7] We are God's servants, not the servants of any government. We are free from all governments and human institutions, because we belong to the owner of the universe and share in that inheritance ("fellow heirs with Christ"). God has made us and bought us for himself.[8]

Being freed from the world and from Caesar, God sends us for a season back into the foreign structures and institutions of society to 'be faithful in that which is another's.' We are to live out the alien

---

5   Mark 12:14-17
6   1 Peter 2:13-14
7   1 Peter 2:16
8   1 Corinthians 6:20

ideas of another kingdom in the midst of our earthly homeland. There will always be tension as we live in these two kingdoms. But God sends us in, not out.

This is stewardship in action. I like to pay the tax that belongs to the government first of all because I love God and want to respect Gods will. Because paying taxes is an act of obedience, this also means I have to be honest in my tax returns. I have to admit that I have not been very faithful to this in the past. There is a great temptation to conceal some income. However, honesty and truth are prerequisites for God's blessing.

Thank God for the income he has provided, although sometimes you think this is not enough. After all, he makes no mistakes! Then thank God for the way in which you can help facilitate the work of the government, in providing necessary services, through your taxes. God provides so that we can also meet the needs of others; this includes all our fellow citizens! Turn your tax return into an offer of thanks to God!

All that this world provides has been entrusted to us by God in stewardship. All that the next world offers has been purchased for us by Another, by Jesus himself through his sacrificial death, for us to make our own in the obedience of faith. As we demonstrate trustworthiness with the material things of this world, so God entrusts to us what truly belongs to us - not that we deserve it, but because God has graced it to us in and through Jesus. To base our lives on this truth is to demonstrate real shrewdness.

Money and mammon in the world's economy

In one way, money does not belong to God, but to the worldly system. Money belongs to the world's economy. Only when it has been redeemed, after we have consecrated all we have under Gods ownership, when we have transferred the money we manage into the Kingdom, does it belong to God.

One of the most famous plays in Western history was penned by the great German writer Johann Wolfgang von Goethe (1749-1832). His two-part drama, Faust, is considered one of the greatest works of German literature. This complicated and sometimes disturbing text tells the story of a young scholar, Faust, who enters into a pact with the devil, in the character of Mephistopheles. In return for Mephistopheles' services to help him realise his ambitions, Faust wagers the devil his soul. Throughout the play, Faust asks Mephistopheles to help him achieve several ostensibly good ends. But each time he summons up the devil's power, Faust gets more than he bargains for!

It looks to me like Mephistopheles is mammon in a not-too-clever disguise!

With his constant companion Mephistopheles, Faust attends the Emperor's court. The empire is in financial ruin through the extravagance of the court, but Mephisto and Faust offer a solution to these problems. Until now, the currency of the empire has been gold, but there is not enough to support the extravagant spending. Mephisto suggests an easy answer - since there is undoubtedly much gold as yet undiscovered beneath the land, which belongs to the Emperor, then surely a promissory note can be made for the value of such gold. He showers the Court with the new paper money. The foundation of the empire has been moved through Mephisto's cunning from the solidity of metallic gold to insubstantial promises on paper.

"To whom it concerns, may you all know, This paper's worth a thousand crowns or so. Such paper's convenient, for rather than a lot of gold and silver, you know what you've got. You've no need of bartering and exchanging, just drown your needs in wine and love-making."

In his Faust part 2, the issuance of paper money does not solve the emperor's spending problems. Instead the ruler and his court become even more extravagant, knowing they can always print more paper money to cover their ever-growing expenses.

The devil has subtly but fundamentally changed the basis of the empire's currency. Instead of being rooted in the solidity offered by a tangible and valued asset, the currency is now based on flimsy paper promises. Thus, long-term monetary stability and powerful restraints on extravagant government spending are sacrificed for short-term gain. The money created belongs to the emperor, but it only leads him into more problems. Thus, the world has created money, not God! God created gold and silver, but not our monetary system. That belongs to the world economy. After all, God does not need it at all! He wants us to use it in the world system as a means of exchange, to test our faithfulness, and as part of our testimony to the world.

Goethe's insights go to the heart of some of our most intractable, long-term economic problems. This has led to the creation of free money, governments printing vast amounts of paper money. Money has never been so cheap. From an economic perspective, the printing press is not necessary, as the creation of money primarily shows up electronically on the central bank's balance sheet, on its accounts.

Money is not backed up by anything real or tangible. The gold standard was abandoned long ago. Money is only worth what the banks think it is worth. Our current money is called fiat money. Fiat money is the opposite of honest money. Fiat money is money that is declared to have value even if it does not. Honest money has value regardless of what people say. In this sense, the worlds money system cannot belong to God. It belongs to another and is controlled by another - mammon.

Still Jesus says that we must be faithful in using 'that which belongs to another.' We must use money wisely and be shrewd in all our dealings. This means using money to benefit people; to help them grow and reach their full potential and to use money in line with Biblical principles as God wishes.

We need a strong economy in which money plays its part as a medium of exchange and must never be an end in itself. This can only be built on what God has created, which is true wealth - human, natural and relational capital. That is, land, agriculture, real resources such as precious metals and the honest, industrial application of human talent and ingenuity to create value.

Jesus unmasked the real power behind money when he said "You cannot serve both God and mammon." Goethe adequately described the work of mammon in our economy through his character Mephistopheles, who caused overspending, loss of trust and financial chaos.

Use according to the rules

Let us study what the driving force behind money is. Jesus is very clear about this. "Show me a coin. Whose face is on the coin? And what is the answer? Caesar's face is on the coin. And then Jesus says, "Then give to Caesar what is of Caesar." And in doing so he gave gold and silver a face. As soon as a face was beaten on the gold or silver, it was placed under another authority. It became part of another system. A world system. Money was made by a world system. God took his hands off it and said we should renounce its powers.

The Greek word used here is very strong. It is often translated as 'give', but that does not reflect the real meaning. It can better be described as: 'Let it follow the rules of what it rules'. It is a very strong expression. It says, "make sure you don't break the rules that govern this stuff." We should follow the rules of using money by not allow ourselves to fall under its powers. And give to God what belongs to God. You and I belong to God, we are made by Him according to His image. Very clear.

Money does not belong to God. He surrendered it (of his own free will) to the system of the world. Even if it is made of metals and materials that are made by him. He has chosen to let go of it. That is why Jesus said: "Give to Caesar what belongs to Caesar. There are rules that govern this stuff." The rules are clearly given in God's Word, such as honesty, truthfulness, integrity, fair weights and measures, keeping your word and paying as agreed. However, in the marketplace we often come up against a different morality. Groucho Marx, famous from the film "Monkey Business," is quoted as saying.

"The secret of business is honesty and fair dealing. If you can fake that you've got it made!"

When we do not follow Gods rules in the marketplace, we place ourselves under the influence of mammon, opening a door for the monkey to work in our lives.

THE MONKEY AND THE ORGAN GRINDER

11

Luke 16:13 "No servant can serve two masters, for either he will hate the one and love the other, or he will be devoted to the one and despise the other. You cannot serve God and money."

Sir Winston Churchill said, "Never listen to the monkey when the organ grinder is in the room!

In former times, organ grinders were street entertainers who played barrel organs. Sometimes they had a monkey that performed to the music.

If you call someone the organ grinder's monkey, you mean that they are doing what a powerful person wants them to do but have no real power themselves. He's the organ grinder's monkey, his only role in life to get money for his boss. People use the terms organ grinder and monkey in many different structures to mean the powerful person and the person who does what they want. Why bother with monkeys when you can deal with the organ grinder?

We focus too much attention on the monkey - mammon, whilst neglecting the Organ Grinder - God Himself!

The emphasis of Jesus' words here falls on the power of mammon to claim, not just our allegiance, but our slave-like devotion and our worship. After all that Jesus has explained in the previous part of the chapter, it is obvious that any two-masters pattern of living is impossible - 'No servant can ... You cannot .... ' We still try, but we still find it impossible.

We must decide who we will listen to, the Organ Grinder or the monkey.

A few years after the fall of Napoleon in 1818, in economically difficult times, the great English poet Samuel Taylor Coleridge wrote, "What are the prospects of our world? The only thing I know is that Mammon and Belial are the gods of our time - and that neither individual nor nation can serve God and mammon. I see more hope in France than in England! This is what it is all about! You can't serve God and Mammon"[1]

The bottom line is; you cannot serve two masters. The American writer, Logan Pearsall Smith echoed Jesus in his line: "Those who set out to serve both God and mammon soon discover there is no God."[2]

Jesus unmasked mammon

Modern Bible translations use the word 'money' for the original Greek 'mammonas.' A Catholic translation even uses the word 'money devil,' which is more in line with the original meaning.

The origin of the original word "Mammonas" in Aramaic (the language Jesus spoke) comes from a word with the meaning of "permanent" or "that which one can rely on." It is said that Jesus used a play on words saying, 'm'aman' or 'my trust,' using the word 'amen' or 'so be it'. American coins carry the words, 'in God we trust'. If only it was like that! It reminds me of a sign I saw above the bar in an Irish pub. "In God we trust, all the rest pay cash!"

Jesus stated on two occasions. "you cannot serve both God and mammon."[3] During his famous "Sermon on the Mount" and later in our parable, he unmasked this power behind money and gave it

---

1   Collected Works, Vol 4; Part 2: The Friend
2   Afterthoughts, 1931, 'Other people.'
3   Matthew 6:24 and Luke 16:13

a name – mammon. Unfortunately, in a lot of our modern Bible translations, the translators chose to use the word money or wealth and consequently rob us of the force of this statement of Jesus. The original word 'mammon' has been translated away by using the words wealth, or money, instead of 'mammon,' so that we miss the true meaning of what Jesus is warning us about! A trick of mammon to allow him to do his work unnoticed - even in our Bibles!

Mammon is not synonymous with money. God and mammon can never be integrated; but God and money should be! Mammon is the fallen spiritual power behind money, seeking to influence people in the spiritual realm to use money unwisely in the worldly or natural realm. "For our struggle is not against flesh and blood, but against the rulers, against the authorities, against the powers of this dark world and against the spiritual forces of evil in the heavenly realms."[4]

Jesus could have said, more logically, you cannot serve both God and… Caesar … or Baal … or Moloch … or Apollo … or Athena …. all gods which were known and venerated at that time. However, he chose to warn us by unmasking for us a new god, mammon, which is a major competitor for our devotion, the power behind money!

Here Jesus personifies money and considers it a sort of god, which is diametrically opposed to the one true God. However, neither the Jews nor Gentiles of His day knew a god by this name. In other words, Jesus did not use a pagan god to show that one must choose between the true God and a false god. This personification and deification of money also means that it is something that claims divinity. What Jesus is revealing is that money is a power. This term is not to be understood as merely a 'force,' but a 'power' in the specific sense in which it is used in the New Testament.

Mammon's power is something that acts by itself. It has spiritual meaning and direction. Power is never neutral. Money as power orients, moves, and controls. Power is also personal. We must not minimise the weight of the parallel Jesus draws between God and

---

4   Ephesians 6:12

mammon. God as a person and mammon as a person find themselves in conflict.

Mammon, however, is completely opposed to God and wants to thwart God's plans with mankind. Money is his weapon to drive a wedge in relationships between people and between people and God. It is impossible, Jesus said, to serve both. He proposes us a choice; one or the other! There is no way between them. It is about hatred and love; about devotion and contempt, about clinging to one and despising the other. We are dealing with two masters who compete for our dedication and love.

Jesus consciously chose a word, a name to describe the power of money, with deep historical, religious and commercial roots. He wanted to say that the power behind money has its roots in the fall of Lucifer, and therefore has demonic characteristics, directed squarely against God, and aimed at winning people's hearts and minds. Mammon has conquered a bridgehead in the human soul and wants to extend this through our in-built propensity to desire and greed; a word that in the daily Greek of that time meant something like "more and more".

The temptation to serve mammon is not the exclusive territory of the rich and prosperous. The long tentacles of mammon reach down to all levels of society and want to embrace the poor and failures with his temptations.

Jesus gave divine status and properties to money when he unmasked mammon. This god, a driving force behind money, wants to give us direction, seduce us, whisper in our ears about important decisions, tell us that money is the most important motive for decisions, persuade us to take sides with money instead of people and God.

Mammon is thus the 'monkey' ... a troublesome monkey that climbs on our backs and clings to us with the intention of moving us to choose money over God; with the ultimate goal of destroying our relationship with our fellow man and with God Himself.

Double focus

Jesus told us where we should place our treasures and our hearts.

"Do not store up for yourselves treasures on earth, where moth and rust destroy, and where thieves break in and steal. But store up for yourselves treasures in heaven, where moth and rust do not destroy, and where thieves do not break in and steal. For where your treasure is, there your heart will be also. The eye is the lamp of the body. If your eyes are good, your whole body will be full of light. But if your eyes are bad, your whole body will be full of darkness. If then the light within you is darkness, how great is that darkness! No one can serve two masters. Either he will hate the one and love the other, or he will be devoted to the one and despise the other. You cannot serve both God and money (Greek: mammon)"[5]

Jesus presents three groups of two. Two treasures: the present Earth and the future Heaven. Two perspectives: the good eye and the bad eye. Two masters: God and mammon.

Money is only of temporary value - unless it is used, spent and shared with a view toward heavenly treasure. Moths destroy fabric, rust corrodes steel and takes away it's usefulness, and thieves can steal almost anything. Jesus could easily have said, 'fires consume, floods inundate, governments seize, enemies attack, things lose their appeal, investments go sour.' No earthly treasure is immune to deteriorating quickly!

Material things just won't stand the test of time. Christ's primary argument against amassing material wealth isn't that it is morally wrong but simply a poor investment. Financial planners try to convince people to look ahead into the future instead of focusing on today or this month, and to think thirty years from now and introduce us to investments for savings and pensions. Jesus would have us look much further into the future. To be shrewd is to plan with eternity in mind and invest in treasures in heaven.

---

5   Matthew 6:19-24

Then, Jesus talks about the eyes which allow light into our lives. In Jewish culture the bad or 'evil eye' is envious, greedy and selfish. Jesus is asking us to focus instead with a good eye on eternal investments and using money according to Biblical principles. We have a choice; to focus on God and his eternal values or to focus on earthly treasures and mammon's values. If we focus on money, mammon can get on our backs and … monkey see, monkey do!

Jesus then goes on to his unequivocal statement of fact of the necessity to choose between two masters - God or mammon. We need to set one of these on the throne and allow one master to lead, control, guide and provide. In this statement, Jesus is describing money not just as a resource or even a kind of litmus test of character, but as a master.

We have choices to make between the investing in the right treasure, looking at our treasure with the right perspective and serving the right master of our treasure! The very nature of the lordship of Christ is all encompassing.

False god

Dr. Martin Luther King Jr. in a 1953 series of discussions on false gods,[6] said, "I consciously reserved this discussion for the last because the worship of the false god of money has had a much longer history and at many points is far more prevalent than the worship of other false gods. Every age has had those individuals who falsely elevated the economic means by which they lived to the status of ends for which they lived."He goes on to say, 'We have been attempting to stress throughout that a man's God is not his theory about God, picked up on the surface of his mind because he happens to live in the twentieth century, but a man's real God is that to which he gives his ultimate devotion, that unifying loyalty which draws his life together and gives it centrality and singleness of aim."

---

6   https://kinginstitute.stanford.edu/king-papers/documents/false-gods-we-worship

King describes three main consequences of worshipping money. Firstly, it causes us to become focussed on making a living, rather than making a life. "There is the danger in such a system that men will become so involved in the money getting process, that they will unconsciously forget to pursue those great eternal values which make life worth living."

Secondly, the tragic attitude of worshipping money leads to selfishness. "The individual who really worships money will seek to get it at any cost and has no concern for the welfare of others."

Lastly, King says that the deification of money causes men to lose their ideals. "They will compromise with honour and principle, keep silent when they should speak out, and engage in sharp practices that are morally degrading and socially pernicious; for money, parents will constrain their daughters into loveless marriages; for money, public officials will sanction crime; for money, men will live their lives in the deep valleys of racketeering and gambling; for money, there are those who will sell their bodies and corrupt their souls."

This is a very poignant description of what Paul meant when he wrote to Timothy.[7] "Those who want to get rich fall into temptation and a trap and into many foolish and harmful desires that plunge people into ruin and destruction. For the love of money is a root of all kinds of evil. Some people, eager for money, have wandered from the faith and pierced themselves with many griefs."

In making the statement "You cannot serve both God and mammon," Jesus is not referring to using or possessing money. In its proper place, used correctly, it can be our servant to benefit life. However, when its importance is magnified to the status of a god, its power corrupts and becomes an instrument to use people to its own ends.

Making money into our god, opens the door for mammon to walk in and torment us. The English novelist and dramatist, Henry Fielding wrote, "If you make money your god, it will plague you like the devil."

---

7   1 Timothy 6:9,10

Serving

We are called to serve God and not money. A penetrating description of serving God as a faithful servant is found in Paul's writing, when he states, "This is how one should regard us, as servants of Christ and stewards of the mysteries of God. Moreover, it is required of stewards that they be found faithful."[8]

The word Paul uses for 'servants' is the Greek '*hupereeretas*' which is used for under-rowers in a Roman galley. The masters up on top determine the direction, pace and leadership, while the slaves on the benches down-under in the boat do all the hard work rowing the boat to a constant drumbeat. A faithful steward is therefore an 'under rower,' someone totally submitted to the master, willing to pull on the oars and work hard, under his direction, pace and leadership. Sometimes, I must, as an 'under rower,' in the lower reaches of a kind of Roman galley, be willing to accept all the world above me throws on my head! That is our assignment! To serve, no matter what the cost.

In the 'upper room', just before the Last Supper, Jesus washed his disciple's feet. I can imagine they had not been cleaned before the evening started and were probably filthy with dust and grime. He, the Son of God, demonstrated true servanthood. John describes the occurrence.[9] Jesus knew, "all things had been given into His hands."

Knowing that he had received all authority and the blessing of God in all he did, empowered him to demonstrate this fulfilling of his mission, "the Son of man did not come to be served, but to serve."[10]

Furthermore, we are to be faithful stewards of the mysteries of God. Well it was certainly a mystery for our manager why he was being unjustly dismissed from his job! It was also a mystery what he was to do in his new circumstances. Managing difficult circumstances and change means looking to God first, who is the provider of all

---

8   1 Corinthians 4:1,2
9   John 13:3-10
10   Mark 10:45

we need, and who will give us the strength to be content and find joy in any circumstance. Undeserved suffering is a great mystery. A loved one may be taken away from us, economic circumstances can cause suffering and living can harm your health! Who can explain why Bach became blind or Beethoven lost his hearing? And yet, from the discipline developed from these infirmities, their talents were developed for our benefits.

Our manager was found to be faithful not because he fought his case with the owner, or tried to wriggle out of the accusations, but because he did something about it. We can be sure that God knows the situations we get into and that He will use them for our benefits because He loves us[11] and will use all circumstances for His plans.

Being a good steward of the mysteries of God means having to learn His ways of communicating to and leading people. We need to know his Word which 'equips us for every good work.'[12].

Money is a great servant but a terrible master

The Christian is given the high calling of using mammon without serving mammon. We are using mammon when we allow God to determine our economic decisions. We are serving mammon when we allow mammon to determine our economic decisions. We simply must decide who is going to make our decisions--- God or mammon. When we make a decision, which is solely and completely money-focussed, we are serving the wrong master. Other considerations must come first. If I know that God wants me to do something and I say, "I can't afford it", then I am neglecting the source of provision. God will pay for everything He orders!

Do we buy a particular home on the basis of the call of God, or because of the availability of money? Do we buy a new car because

---

11   Genesis 50:20
12   2 Timothy 3;16

we can afford it, or because God instructed us to buy a new car? If money determines what we do or do not do, then money is our boss. If God determines what we do or do not do, then God is our boss. My money might say to me, 'You have enough to buy that,' but my God might say to me, 'I don't want you to have it.' Now, who am I to obey? Most of us allow money to dictate our decisions: what kind of house we live in, what vacation we will take, what job we will hold. Money decides.

J. Hudson Taylor would never have launched the great chapter in mission history called the China Inland Mission if he had let money decide. He was an ordinary person with few resources, yet once he had determined that God wanted him to go, he went. God had made the decision, not money. His master was God, and it was this master that he served.

Over the course of his effective ministry, God channelled very large sums of money through Hudson Taylor, enough to care for the needs of well over a thousand missionaries. But from his earliest days in the slums of London, Taylor had learned to understand money in the light of the cross. He had learned to use money without serving it.

Throughout his career, Luther fought against what he saw as the two-sided coin of 'mammonism," both the ascetic flight from money and the acquisitive drive for it. His foundation for this battle was the great reversal of the gospel that a person's worth is not determined by what he or she does or does not possess, but rather by God's promise in Christ. Thus, money is not the lord of life, but the gift of God to be used for worshipping Him, serving our neighbour and building up our community.

Martin Luther observed: "Many a one thinks that he has God and everything in abundance when he has money and possessions; he trusts in them and boasts of them with such firmness and assurance as to care for no one. Lo, such a man also has a god, mammon by name, which is money and possessions, on which he sets all his heart, and which is also the most common idol on earth."

What Luther denounces here is actually not the possession of money or property but the human heart's misdirected trust in it, transforming possession into a divine entity and relying on it as if money could satisfy the most urgent need and provide security, protection and total care. Luther, however, warns that we should not become attached to our earthly possessions, but use, administer and possess them "as if we possessed not"[13]

Mammon wants to tie us up in the world. C.S. Lewis observed, "Prosperity knits a man to the World. He feels that he is 'finding his place in it,' while really it is finding its place in him. His increasing reputation, his widening circle of acquaintances, his sense of importance, the growing pressure of absorbing and agreeable work, build up in him a sense of being really at home in earth[14]."

Serving mammon?

What are some symptoms of mammon influence? Here are ten symptoms which can give an indication of the influence of mammon in my life. (Give each statement a score: 0 = This is really me and 10 = I don't recognise this at all):

1. Worry (I am unrestful and get agitated about money)

2. Financial disorder (I don't know where my money goes)

3. A structural financial deficit (I am always short of cash)

4. False economies (I cannot afford it, but I know I should)

5. Impulsive purchasing behaviour (I just cannot pass on this opportunity)

6. Stinginess (I cannot afford to give)

7. Greed (I can never say that this is enough)

---

13   1 Corinthians 7:29-31

14   C.S. Lewis, "The Screwtape Letters." , p 143

8. Dissatisfaction (other people have more than me, and that's not fair)

9. Over-indebtedness (I can't afford the payments)

10. Overestimating the power of money (with enough money, I can do anything I want)

What strikes you about your answers? To what extent are you or have you been sensitive to mammon? Is there anything which, on looking back, you are thankful for, or for which you are ashamed, sorry for or want to confess? What are you going to do about it? On which of the above 10 points would you like to improve, change?

THE HIGHER A MONKEY CLIMBS...

12

Luke 16:14 "The Pharisees, who were lovers of money, heard all these things, and they ridiculed him."

Donald Rumsfeld, Secretary of Defence under George W. Bush up to 2006, quoted second world war General Joe Stilwell, "The higher a monkey climbs, the more you see of its behind!" When someone gets too serious about their importance, you see how much they miss the reality of who they really are.

Well, the Pharisees were full of their own importance and righteousness. Climbing the ladder of importance, influence, public acknowledgment and riches, you could see their backsides - and it was not a pretty sight!

Seneca, the Greek philosopher said, "The longer the rich man extends his colonnades, the higher he lifts his towers, the wider he stretches out his mansions, the deeper he digs his caverns for summer, the huger loom the roofs of the banquet-halls he rears, so much the more there will be to hide heaven from his sight."

Jesus' radically different approach to material things, was as uncomfortably challenging in those days as it is in today's frenetic marketplace. Luke tells us that, amongst those listening in on this teaching, were some of the Pharisees. These highly moral and religiously orthodox people crop up frequently in the Gospels, mainly as hostile pursuers of Jesus on account of his impact on ordinary folk and his constant undermining of their own influence. Luke here has a fascinating aside about the Pharisees in general, calling them 'lovers of money' . Unless Luke had made this comment, we probably would not have guessed that this was a characteristic of the Pharisees. It might well explain much of the vitriol they directed at Jesus on account of his friendship with wealthy tax collectors. The Pharisees were consumed with envy for tax collectors. They were lovers of money and hooked on getting more and more. These Pharisees, listening to Jesus' teaching about mammon, were derisive about his remarks: 'They ridiculed him.' The word actually means 'they turned up their noses at him'. This fact is a powerful warning for any who find themselves similarly, even if secretly, dismissive of what Jesus has said in this passage about wealth. The shrewdness Jesus recommends may not be in line with received marketplace wisdom, but it goes to the heart of the matter and we ignore it at our peril.

Loving money

The Pharisees controlled quite a large banking operation in Jerusalem. Since very early times, temples had been used as 'safe-havens' for money. In first century Jerusalem, the Temple treasury-bank held not only the wealth of the ruling aristocrats, but also the surplus funds of the city's middle class and numerous traders and craftsmen; temple funds were invested for commercial purposes. The commercial activity that centred on the Temple cult provided the majority of the city's annual income. The temple was undergoing a huge building project. The Roman chronicler Josephus tells us that Herod the Great employed more than 10.000 workmen and 1.000 priests in the Temple area at that time.

When Jesus interrupted the commercial exchanges in the Temple, driving out money-changers, this was not just a theological challenge, but brought him into conflict with the commercial interests of the Pharisees, which were enormous! The Temple dominated the skyline of Jerusalem, and dominated the city's economy, the temple cult providing the main source of income for the people of the city.

The Temple banking operation was so rich, that Josephus describes the loot taken by the Roman Emperor Vespasian and his son Titus after the destruction of the Temple in AD 70, as 'fifty tons of gold and silver.' This was taken back to Rome and used to finance the Colosseum.

Eckhard and Wolfgang Stegemann compared first century Jerusalem with modern Switzerland. "Manifold privileges had made the Jerusalem Temple the safest bank in the Middle East. In the investment area, it enjoyed a respect like that of Switzerland today. Many foreigners, merchants and politicians held accounts there – a lucrative business for the Temple bank, due to the deposit taxes it levied."

Another indication of the wealth of the Temple is given by Josephus describing Crassus (a financial advisor to Caesar), 'who plundered the treasury of the Temple, carrying off 8,000 talents of gold and 2,000 talents of silver that Pompey had left in the treasury."[1] A talent was worth 6,000 denarii and a denarius a day's wage. Today, that would be bank assets equivalent to a value of around 6 billion US dollars. Mammon was very firmly entrenched in the Temple banking system.

No wonder that Peter, at the end of his first sermon cried out, "Save yourselves from this crooked generation."[2]

The Pharisees were highly educated people with an extraordinarily thorough knowledge of God's Word, but they did not understand Jesus and even insulted him. Although they were very religious and said to be 'god-fearing', they ignored God's words and were at the mercy of mammon. Despite their proud attitude, Jesus could look straight through them for who they really were. Their true nature was exposed, and Jesus saw through their pronounced self-righteousness and revealed their ugly side. They are simply concerned with power and material things. The monkey appears clinging to the backs of the Pharisees!

---

1 Josephus, Antiquities 14.78, 105-110

2 Acts 2:40

Until Luke told us this, we could hardly have deduced this from the earlier stories about the Pharisees. It explains why they bombarded Jesus with remarks about his friendship with wealthy tax inspectors! The London City banker, Stephen Green, remarked, "On the whole, jealousy is a weapon that mammon uses to enslave those who don't have money and those who do." The Pharisees were obsessed with jealousy towards the tax inspectors. They were lovers of money, as much in the spell of raising money as Zacchaeus. Therefore, when they heard Jesus on the subject of money, they ridiculed him and raised their noses to him.

They were blinded by money and could not see Jesus for whom he was. This blindness was reinforced by their legal approach to the giving of alms, because they fulfilled their religious duty, they received God's approval. Jesus reminded them that God wanted to deal with the avarice of their hearts.

Oscar Wilde wrote the novel "The Portrait of Dorian Gray" in 1890. Dorian Gray is a handsome, naive young man and a friend of a painter who makes a perfect portrait of him. Dorian wishes that he would always remain so beautiful, and that the painting in his place would become older. Despite his unhealthy behaviour, his physical appearance remains youthful and unmarked by dissolute life. However, his portrait catalogues every evil deed by turning his once handsome features in the portrait into a hideous, grotesque mask.

During the next 18 years Dorian becomes more and more malicious, but his appearance remains the same. However, the Dorian in the painting becomes older and uglier, until he has become unrecognisable. Eventually he becomes angry with the painting and stabs the portrait with a knife. In the room his housekeeper finds the painting, which has been changed back to its original state. On the floor next to it is Dorian's body, which has been stabbed and turned into an ugly old man. His appearance did not reflect his corrupt heart, but leads in the end to ugliness and corruption. This describes the Pharisees quite well.

Jesus took a tough stand against the hypocritical Pharisees: "Woe betide you, Scriptures and Pharisees, hypocrites, you resemble whitewashed tombs, which look beautiful from outside, but are full of bones of death and other impurities."[3]

A focus on money, although the outward appearance seems to be quite beautiful, can eat us up from within and turn our lives ugly.

Eventually, instead of loving money, we end up loving the power behind it. In 1909, the painter Evelyn de Morgan, expressed this in a painting in which a woman is seen standing at the feet of mammon. In the painting, the woman has decided to turn her back on God and serve mammon, she clutches desperately at the knee of mammon, and looks longingly up into his face, which stares down at her remorselessly. Mammon holds out a bag of gold, but the woman ignores the money. She has moved from the love of gold, to the love of mammon himself and so has cut herself off from the love of God and sold herself to mammon.

De Morgan commented on the painting;

> "The woman turned her back on God and clings to
> mammon…
> Mammon offers her gold,but she no longer desires the
> gold …
> but mammon himself … and she is doomed!"

Greed is good

The apostle Paul coined that much quoted (and often misquoted) saying 'The love of money is the root of all evil'.[4] This contains the same Greek word that is here used to describe the Pharisees. The word comes again in a long list of behaviour patterns in another of Paul's personal letters to Timothy. There he is describing the general characteristics of a society or a generation that has jettisoned fundamental values.

---

3   Matt 23:27
4   1 Timothy 6: 10

"But mark this: There will be terrible times in the last days. People will be lovers of themselves, lovers of money, boastful, proud, abusive, disobedient to their parents, ungrateful, unholy, without love, unforgiving, slanderous, without self-control, brutal, not lovers of the good, treacherous, rash, conceited, lovers of pleasure rather than lovers of God— having a form of godliness but denying its power. Have nothing to do with such people."[5]

It is a list which is too close to our contemporary world for comfort. No society anywhere is irretrievably and universally corrupt like that, but these trends have been gradually rising to the surface in the last thirty years, not least in the way practitioners in the financial markets operate.

In Oliver Stone's classic 1987 film about Wall Street, the anti-hero Gordon Gecko (Michael Douglas), said to the shareholders of Teldar Paper, "Greed is right. Greed works. Greed clarifies, cuts through, and captures the essence of the evolutionary spirit. Greed, in all of its forms - greed for life, for money, for love, knowledge - has marked the upward surge of mankind. And greed - you mark my words - will not only save Teldar Paper, but that other malfunctioning corporation called the USA." This was characteristic of the Reagan-Thatcher 'boom years' of the unbridled capitalism of the nineties.

In September 2009, former Harvard Business School graduate, Philip Delves Broughton, now a writer for the London Evening Standard, observed, "Gekko's 'Greed is Good' speech in the film 'Wall Street' is still shown to MBA students at business schools. It is intended as a morality lesson but ends up feeling more like a pep talk. At my old business school, Harvard, Gekko's speech electrified a snoozy morning class on leadership. By the time Gekko was done berating the board of Teldar Paper, the entire class was grinning and alert."

I really enjoyed the sequel to the film, Wall Street 2. In this Gordon Gecko is out of prison and addresses students about greed.

---

5   2 Timothy 3:-15

"Someone reminded me the other day that I once said, greed is good. Well it appears greed is not only good, it is legal. We are all drinking the same cool-aid.

But it is greed that makes my bartender buy three houses, he cannot afford with no money down. And it is greed that makes your parents refinance their 200,000-dollar mortgage for 250,000 dollars. Now they take that extra 50,000 dollars and go to the shopping mall, so they can buy a new plasma TV, cell phones, computers and an SUV. And hey, why not a second home while we are at it. Gee Wiz, we all know the prices of houses in America always go up. Right? It is greed that makes the government of this country cut the interest rates to 1% after 9/11 so we can all go shopping again.

They got all these fancy names for trillions of dollars for credit, CMO, CDO, SIV, ABS. You know I honestly think there are only 75 people in the world that know what they are. But I will tell you what they are, they are WMDs; Weapons of Mass Destruction. When I was away, it seemed that greed, got greedier. With a little bit of envy mixed in. Hedge fund managers came home with 50 to 100 million bucks a year. So Mr. Banker, he looks around and says. 'My life looks pretty boring'. So he starts leveraging his interest up to 40%, 50% to 100%. With your money not his. Yours. Because he could. You are supposed to be borrowing, not them. And the beauty of the deal is no one is responsible."

Warren Buffett quipped: "You won't encounter much traffic taking the high road on Wall Street!"

Greed is never good, nor does it serve to work any good purpose. Since we will never be able to attain everything we desire, greed offers us dissatisfaction. Our greediness ultimately destroys us as we harden our hearts, ignoring the needs of others. Ultimately, greed motivates us to pursue poor choices that plunge us into destruction. "A greedy person tries to get rich quick, but it only leads to poverty."[6]

---

6   Proverbs 28:20

The practice of generosity protects us from the deadly effects of greed. Israel's Jordan River remains a source of life as it flows into the Sea of Galilee and then travels to the Dead Sea. In all likelihood, Paul witnessed first-hand the Sea of Galilee's generous giving as it irrigates fruitful fields and provides abundant fishing resources. In contrast, the Dead Sea has no outlet, greedily robbing the arid region of moisture. Both man and animal refuse to drink from its acrid waters. It contains no life of any sort, except a few kinds of microbes - fish placed into its waters die rapidly. Greed causes our lives to also become foul before God. But a life that flows abundantly shares all that God has given us. When we give, we truly prosper and are refreshed.[7]

We can more readily see, I believe, why Jesus was so adamant about the power of mammon. Richard Foster refers to 'the tough old miser within and the spiritual powers without'.[8] Mammon's power operates in both ways, something the Pharisees failed to appreciate because 'the tough old miser' ruled within them and they could not recognise it. It is likely that this blindness was reinforced, if not actually caused, by their legalistic approach to almsgiving - because they majored on this religious duty, they concluded that they were approved by God. They saw giving to charity as the extent of their obligations in this regard, but Jesus reminds them that God wants to tackle the greed in their hearts - a reality that no amount of charitable giving can begin to touch.

In almost the entire Western cultural history greed was seen as a destructive and sinful characteristic. Greek mythology tells of King Midas who, after he had been allowed to make a wish from the god Dionysos, wanted everything he touched to turn into gold. Food, drink, even his own children were turned into gold as soon as Midas touched them; the king begged the gods to forgive him for his greed.

The great English poet William Wordsworth wrote on the 1842 bond default of Pennsylvania, which still hadn't paid off bondholders (like

---

7   Proverbs 11:24–25

8   Richard Foster, Money, Sex and Power, Hodder and Stoughton, 1985, p.58

Wordsworth, presumably) when he wrote "To the Pennsylvanians" ("Sonnet from a Surly Creditor,") in 1845. These words lament the movement away from the Quaker principles of William Penn to a culture of dishonour and injustice.

> "Grieve for the land on whose wild woods his name
> Was fondly grafted with a virtuous aim,
> Renounced, abandoned by degenerate Men
> For state-dishonour black as ever came
> To upper air from Mammon's loathsome den."

Judas in me?

As I read the Bible, I find myself periodically identifying with the life or behaviour of a specific Bible character; David, Moses, Joseph, Paul - heroes of the faith. Sometimes, I identify with their good qualities and sometimes with their bad ones. However, until challenged one day, Judas was never one of them. Yet, in reflection, I discovered that there is more of Judas in me than I would ever like to admit.

While attending a conference, one of the main speakers made a passing comment in his presentation that sent shivers down my spine. The speaker said, "Judas betrayed Jesus for money". For the first time in my entire life I found myself painfully identifying with Judas, the betrayer.

I have often related to Peter, too bold and carelessly impetuous, and to Samson, with his great strength, but lack of self-control, and even to King Saul, who 'played the fool.' But never before have I ever seen myself in Judas, the betrayer – until that moment.

What exactly does it mean to "betray" someone? The word "betray" means to "turn someone over to another," the way a police officer would turn over a convict to a prison warden. I asked myself, "Has my life or my behaviour ever turned Jesus over to be mocked, ridiculed, or punished by another because of my hypocritical, uncontrolled, self-centred life?"

In business, I have, to my shame, done things which did not bring honour to God, because of a more urgent need for money, and was a traitor to God. I hate to think what others would think about the Jesus I serve.

Judas didn't kill Jesus, he only set Him up to be killed by others. When Jesus chose his disciples, Luke said that Judas would become a "traitor"[9] – meaning "someone who is false to a duty or an obligation." None of us would like to think of ourselves as traitors to Christ. But think about it. Have you ever been inconsistent in a duty or an obligation to Christ because his will and your will didn't align? Have you ever abandoned his business for your own because your business looked more profitable? Have you ever been guilty of dereliction of duty to him in your financial dealings with others? These sobering questions may bring to mind times in which you have indeed been a traitor to him.

Cyrpian, Bishop of North Africa in the third century, wrote in his 'De Lapsis' on the fall of the church leaders in his days, as a result of mammon influence.

"Each one was intent on adding to his inheritance. Forgetting what the faithful used to do under the Apostles and what they should always be doing, each one with insatiable greed was absorbed in adding to his wealth. Gone was the devotion of bishops to the service of God, gone was the clergy's faithful integrity, gone the generous compassion for the needy, gone all discipline in our behaviour. What subtle tricks to deceive the hearts of the simple, what sly manoeuvres to entrap the brethren! … Too many bishops, instead of giving encouragement and example to others, made no account of the ministration which God had entrusted to them, and took up the administration of secular business: they left their sees, abandoned their people, and toured the markets in other territories on the look-out for profitable deals. If that is what we have become, what do we not deserve for such sins…?"

---

9   Luke 6:16

We need to be constantly on guard and alert to mammon's tricks, otherwise we can so easily become a traitor to our assignment.

A MONKEY IN SILK...

Luke 16:15 And he said to them, "You are those who justify yourselves before men, but God knows your hearts. For what is exalted among men is an abomination in the sight of God."

The saying, 'A monkey in silk is a monkey no less,' means no matter how someone dresses, it's the same person underneath. Or, 'Don't judge a book by its cover.' Italians say, 'It's not the clothes that make the monk." The appearance does not always say the truth about a person. This is certainly true of our monkey - mammon. The devil is the father of lies and a master of deception. All his servants exist to feed this monster. Mammon makes promises which may seem attractive but are empty and without substance in bringing us the true riches which come out of a daily relationship with Jesus. The Pharisees were concerned only with external things and self-justification. They were certainly not what they wanted us to think of them. God hates people who build their lives on self-righteousness, because it makes the sacrifice of the Cross of Christ to become irrelevant.

Justifying ourselves

What Jesus says to the Pharisees is this: "You live to justify yourselves before men, but God knows your hearts; for what is highly prized by people is an abomination in the sight of God". The major concerns of these Pharisees were appearances, reputations, status and external things. They worked desperately to convince everyone that they were God's approved elite. As far as material wealth was concerned, they were no paupers - however much they may have coveted the kind of riches amassed by tax collectors. The Pharisees claimed that their wealth was God's reward for their piety and this pride was what Jesus aimed to rectify. His reference to 'what is highly esteemed among men' focuses on what the Pharisees counted so important, that is, appearances, reputations, externals, wealth.

Their entire lifestyle was absorbed with these matters. It amounted to an elaborate attempt at self-justification, as though these things were of supreme significance. And the Pharisees put it about that this is what mattered to God; that God was impressed and pleased with such self-justifying behaviour. This is what Jesus calls 'an abomination in the sight of God'; basing our lives on the image and the reputation we build up with our material possessions. This is aggravated when we kid ourselves that God's blessing rests on us, while we resist any approaches he makes to get underneath the surface and tackle the greed in our hearts.

The Bible teacher, Selwyn Lloyd says, "Take it from someone who has had a lifetime of experience of trying to help Christians understand their relationship to their finances - money has a very powerful and profound effect upon the human soul. I have watched hundreds of Christians in my time become financially blessed and then develop an acquisitive streak that in turn makes their souls as metallic as the coins they seek."

Someone has said, "Having a good deal of money does not change a person, it merely unmasks them." If a person is naturally selfish or greedy, money will simply show up those tendencies in a greater and clearer light. It is sad how the longing for money can create a fever in the soul.

Jacques Ellul explains: 'Grace must invade the power of money, for when mammon is destroyed by grace, it is no longer a formidable power'[1] . The Pharisees spent their time and their money trying to justify themselves, whereas the only way to true justification is by God's grace in forgiveness.

This is what Jesus consistently demonstrated and it is the fundamental reason for the hostility of the Pharisees towards him. Jesus and the Pharisees proclaimed different messages about God and his kingdom. This radical difference was nowhere more apparent than in their respective attitudes to money. Jesus majored on grace and giving, the Pharisees were hooked on greed and getting.

The heart

The Pharisees were concerned about their external image and reputation and worked hard to convince people that they were God's elected representatives. Mammon wants us to believe that outward appearances and the opinions of others are the most important and that material success would be proof of this.

Jesus says that God is horrified about this, calling it 'an abomination,' something which gives disgust or hatred. Money, possessions, prestige and power are not necessarily signs of God's blessing! God can just as well bless us by taking things away from us!

It has happened to me at least three times that a successful project ended abruptly. Things went well, contracts were in place and, like the rich businessman from Lucas 12, I thought I was saying to myself, "You have a lot of goods in stock, enough for many years! Take rest, eat, drink and enjoy yourself!" Instead of gaining even more, and being able to enjoy my new position, God led the circumstances in such a way that I had to leave that enterprise behind me because he wanted to put me on a different track. With hindsight I am very happy that he did this!

John of Antiochia lived in the 4th. Century A.D. and became known worldwide as John Chrystostomos (the name means golden-

---

1   Money and Power, page 75

mouthed), Bishop of Constantinople, at a time of unprecedented prosperity. He wrote, "Wealth misappropriates your thinking to the most intensive degree." He described some of his rich contemporaries; 'Their thinking is a kind of citadel, possessed by the love of money'. He wrote about the damage that mammon caused to the people in his grip," the wound is in the most vital parts".[2]

The Bible says that, 'The heart is deceitful above all things and beyond cure. Who can understand it?"[3] In the law of Moses, as indeed in the Bible as a whole, there is much stress laid on outward behaviour and how we are to treat our neighbours. Yet the Mosaic law is clear that mere external conformity to its demands is insufficient.

The Lord demands an obedience that goes far deeper than that. His standards must be on our heart—they must impact our motives, thinking, emotions, and everything else that we are, both inside and out.[4] This is a hard truth to grasp, which is why God emphasises it from the beginning of His dealings with the people of Israel. The Bible emphasises the need for a circumcised heart that is set apart to love the Lord above all else.

This is a huge reason why handling money Gods way is so important. Jesus gave us a very insightful principle about the connection between your money and your heart, "For where your treasure is, there your heart will be also."[5] Some years ago an old mentor of mine asked me a very penetrating question. "Peter, is God the most important in your life?" "Yes, of course," I replied. "Well, then. Show me your bank statements and I will tell you what is the most important in your life." This shocked me as he explained that we spend money according to the priorities of the heart, on that which we value the most. "If the importance of your relationship with God is not reflected in your spending, then you are fooling yourself," he said.

---

2   The gospel in Solentiname, Vol1. Ernesto Cardenal, p. 22.
3   Jeremiah 17:9
4   Deuteronomy 6:6
5   Matthew 6:21

He went on to say, "if you want a heart for the gospel, spend your money on missions. If you want a heart for the church, spend your money there." It is so true that our heart also follows our money. Reflecting on times when I invested in a share portfolio, I remember looking at the market prices several times a day!

Overcoming mammon

In overcoming mammon, four words seem to me to be essential. Decide, dethrone, desacralise and depart from it.

Decide

A decision is needed - serve God or serve mammon. Most Christians have never been faced with such a decision, which I believe is a one-time major life decision, followed by daily obedience and devotion to following Gods ways of handling money. This decision could be likened to baptism. A one-time event followed by daily following Jesus. The great Reformer, Martin Luther, once wrote that "there are three conversions necessary: the conversion of the heart, the conversion of the mind, and the conversion of the purse. Of these three, it may well be that we find the conversion of the purse to be the most difficult."

Charles Spurgeon writes, "With some (Christians) the last part of their nature that ever gets sanctified is their wallets."

The story is told of Sam Houston, hero of Texas history, who gave his life to the Lord in the later years of life and asked to be baptised. He was taken down to a little country stream, and the pastor said, "General Houston, you should take your glasses off because I am going to immerse you in water." There also were some papers in General Houston's pocket, so he took those out as well.

Then, just as he was getting ready to go into the water, the pastor noticed that General Houston still had his wallet in his back pocket. He said, "Well, General, you might want to take that wallet out of your pants. It is going to get wet."

Houston responded, "If there is any part of me that needs baptising, it is my wallet." So Houston was baptised, wallet and all.

Dethrone.

Then, we need to dethrone mammon in our lives.

Recognising Jesus' victory over mammon at the cross, taking this cross up daily, living out of Jesus' victory will break the power of mammon in our lives, "by cancelling the record of debt that stood against us with its legal demands. This he set aside, nailing it to the cross. He disarmed the rulers and authorities and put them to open shame, by triumphing over them in him."[6] Jesus broke the power of money by allowing himself to be sold as a slave to the world system and to be bought by the Pharisees, thereby breaking this power of buying and selling to set us free!

When we consciously transfer all that we possess into God's hands, and accept His ownership of all things, we take mammon off the throne and take away his leadership and influence over our finances. If you have transferred everything to God, then nothing belongs to mammon and all possessions and money fall under Gods control.

Abraham was asked to sacrifice his son, Isaac. And I can well imagine that by the time he came down from the mountain, the words 'my and mine' had forever changed their meaning for him. The apostle Paul speaks of 'having nothing, and yet possessing everything.'[7] As we enter the school of inner renunciation we come into that state in which nothing belongs to us and yet everything is available to us.

We badly need a conversion in our understanding of ownership. Perhaps we need to stamp everything in our possession with the reminder 'Given by God, owned by God, and to be used for the purposes of God.' We need to find ways to remind ourselves over and over again that the earth is the Lord's, not ours.

------

6   Colossians 2:14,15
7   2 Corinthians 6:10

Desacralise

Then, we need to desacralise money by taking away it's sacred, holy powers. Money must never be a goal in itself and become an idol.

We desacralise money by giving the first and best part of all income and moving money into Gods economy! Then the work of mammon, the spoiler, will be negated.

"Bring the full tithe into the storehouse, that there may be food in my house. And thereby put me to the test, says the Lord of hosts, if I will not open the windows of heaven for you and pour down for you a blessing until there is no more need. I will rebuke the devourer for you, so that it will not destroy the fruits of your soil, and your vine in the field shall not fail to bear, says the Lord of hosts."[8] The 'devourer', mammon, can no longer spoil Gods plans for us.

We desacralise money by bringing grace into the world of buying and selling. God receives the money which is given and brings it into His economy … and from this storehouse, He will supply. An example of this is giving to the poor. "Whoever is kind to the poor lends to the Lord, and he will reward them for what they have done."[9] The rich, young ruler did not understand this. When asked by Jesus to sell up and give everything to the poor, he went away sad, because he was very rich, and he missed Jesus' offer of eternal life. He didn't realise that giving to the poor was lending to the Lord, who would repay![10]

Give with a glad and generous heart. Giving has a way of routing out the 'tough old miser' within us. Even the poor need to know that they can give. Just the very act of letting go of money, or some other treasure, does something within us. It destroys the demon greed.

Some will be led, like Saint Francis of Assisi, to give away everything and embrace 'Lady Poverty.' That is not a command for all, but it is the word of the Lord for some to live a very simple life, as Jesus'

---

8   Malachi 3:10,11a
9   Proverbs 19:17
10   Proverbs 19:17

encounter with the rich young ruler testifies. We must not despise people called to this form of giving but rejoice with them in their growing freedom from the god mammon.

Giving is winning a victory over the dark powers that seek to control and oppress us. The powers that energise money cannot abide that very unnatural of acts - giving. Money is made for taking, for bargaining, for manipulating, but not for giving. This is exactly why giving has such ability to defeat the powers of money.

Depart

Lastly, we must depart from it. We depart from it, when we recognise that we want to follow God's principles of managing money instead of being influenced by mammon. We must repent and accept God's forgiveness and cleansing from mammon interference. "If we confess our sins, he is faithful and just to forgive us our sins and to cleanse us from all unrighteousness (*adikia*)."[11]

We need to depart from a lifestyle which is centred on money and possessions and practice a lifestyle of simplicity. A good starting point is to answer the question for yourself, "How much is enough?" How much is enough for your current responsibilities, in the economic strata God has called you to?

We need to depart from valuing what we measure. This means demonetarising our values. A Harvard Business Review article stated, "You are what you measure." How can you measure joy, contentment, peace, loyalty, goodness, faithfulness?

Success in business seems to be determined by measurables such as sales, profitability, productivity. Departing from a money driven purpose of business means departing from profit maximisation to put the wellbeing of the employee first; to serve the customer in the best possible way; to look after the creation.

––––––––––––––––

11   1 John 1:9

Success in life seems to be determined by measurables like salary, possessions, bank balances. Departing from money driven values means focussing on love, friendship, freedom. The world crowns success; God crowns faithfulness!

Value for money must never be the only measure. Our parable teaches us the value of developing relationships, and this can sometimes be costly! In the final analysis, the real measure of your wealth is how much you'd be worth if you lose all your money!

Realise that mammon is a little thing, who has been overcome and quakes at the Word of God. But remember, you can get the monkey off your back, by invoking Jesus' work and God's Word, but the circus does not leave town! Only when Jesus returns and He removes mammon completely, will we be totally free from all temptations!

So step on it. Yell at it. Laugh at it. Spread it around!

GODS MONKEY

14

God's ape

As the god of this age, Satan has set up a complete counterfeit of Christianity. Have you ever gone to the zoo, and stood face to face with an ape? You make a move, and he mimics you. Not without reason did St. Augustine term Satan "Simius Dei," which means "the ape of God."

Martin Luther agreed with St. Augustine and said, that the devil is God's ape.[1] He wrote, "The Greeks and heathens in after times imitated this, and built temples for their idols in certain places, as at Ephesus for Diana, at Delphos for Apollo, etc. For, where God builds a church there the devil would also build a chapel. They imitated the Jews also in this, namely, that as the Most Holiest was dark, and had no light, even so and after the same manner, did they make their shrines dark where the devil made answer. Thus is the devil ever God's ape."

The great English writer, Daniel Defoe echoed Luther[2],
    "Wherever God erects a house of prayer
    the Devil always builds a chapel there;
    And 't will be found, upon examination,
    the latter has the largest congregation."

---

1   Colloquia Mensalia (1566) ch. 2 (tr. H. Bell as Martin Luther's Divine Discourses, 165
2   Daniel Defoe in 'The True Born Englishman.'

He is certainly right!

Now, Luther didn't mean that the devil was simply a monkey in comparison to God, nor was he thinking that God was some sort of divine organ grinder and the devil was the little monkey on a leash that danced to God's tune and did the ugly side of His will, leaving God to be the "good guy."

He meant that the devil is always copying God—aping God—but doing so in a way that takes God's Word and actions and flips them on their head, putting forth an opposite, yet very appealing form of what God intends and gives; e.g., darkness instead of light; lies instead of truth; prideful independence rather than humble trust in God; and above all things, death instead of life. Mammon, as one of the devil's brigade, is out to copy Gods way of dealing with money - the wrong way! Instead of generosity, greed; instead of freedom, debt; instead of contentment, the fear of never having enough.

Are you being deceived by the "Simius Dei — the ape of God?" Mammon is at work all around us, and on the surface, it looks pretty nice…

The good-looking young banker

When we think of a devil, we automatically conjure up a picture of an ugly, red monster with horns and a forked tail.

However, the Bible describes Satan masquerading as 'an angel of light.'[3] Paul goes on to write, that it is not surprising then, that his servants also masquerade as servants of righteousness. Their end will be what their actions deserve." Mammon certainly puts on an attractive mask for us!

Louis Couperus, is one of Holland's greatest authors. He sketched a masterful picture of the fascinating world around the turn of the last century. He wrote of his apocalyptic vision of mammon appearing in the form of a handsome, young banker.[4]

---

3   2 Corinthians 11:14
4   Haagsche Post, April 14, 1917

"The International Bank of Satan looked very different from any other bank. There were no desks, men writing or ladies typing. In an immense room, which resembled a party hall - really the halls of sin became larger and larger and this sensual pavilion became a Ballroom! – there stood Satan's banker – the young, blond, charming man. He stood laughing on a kind of round, raised throne and in the middle, on the steps to the dais he rested on a row of golden calves; in fact the whole room shone with gold, the walls appeared to be of gold and that shone like mirrors.

The young banker – he was dressed just like any other young banker these days – just stood laughing with arms wide apart and rubbed his fingertips together. Then I saw that many side doors gave entry to Satan's International Bank; truly, it seems as if access was only through these side doors which all opened together, and that through my side door streamed hundreds of creatures with me; they were Europeans, Asians, Americans; creatures from all corners of the earth and they thronged around the raise dais…

"What's he called?", I asked Bel.

"He's called mammon, sir," said Bel, "and he is The Goldfever." The charming mammon chattered to me – he had noticed me and he continued;

"I am the Goldfever! He who worships me, I will sprinkle with gold, cover in gold, heap with gold! Kneel, kneel and worship me!"

He looked so young, so dazzling and radiant and there appeared a strong attraction coming out of him, because the creatures, God's creatures or Satan's creatures, they jostled to get to the steps of mammon's throne, to kneel between the golden calves."

Goethe wrote in his work, Faust about mammon's work. Mammon drives us to 'restless action' on one hand and also makes it easy to live a soft life of self-centred indulgence, "laying the pillow straight,'-making life easy.

> "Cursed Mammon be, when he with treasures
> To restless action spurs our fate!
> Cursed when for soft, indulgent leisures,
> He lays for us the pillows straight."[5]

As Francis Quarles said, "What treasures here do mammon's sons behold! Yet know that all that which glitters is not gold."[6] Mammon's temptations are subtle and, on the surface, attractive. In practice, however, it can all turn out very differently.

Memo from mammon

C.S. Lewis's imaginative classic, "The Screwtape Letters," consists of thirty-one letters from Screwtape, a senior devil in Hell's civil service, addressed to Wormwood, a devil-in-training. The apprentice is charged with tempting a young man - 'the patient' - in order to secure his soul for Hell.

I have no clue as to any possible relationship between Screwtape and mammon … but it looks like they have the very same agenda! I like to think mammon is Satan's banker!

Mammon can only imitate God. Together with his boss, Satan, mammon only knows how to pervert, in a poor imitation, what God does - in uniting believers to him. Satan and his devils absorb on the basis of selfish love, whereas God and His angels replicate on the basis of selfless love. God wants individuals united to him, people remade in his image, yet distinct and fully themselves. The devil is out to remove our individuality, our uniqueness, our very personality.

"Never forget that when we are dealing with any pleasure in its healthy and normal and satisfying form, we are, in a sense, on the

---

5   Faust, Part 1; Scene 4:1599
6   Emblems, Book II. Emblem V.

Enemy's ground," warns Screwtape. "He made the pleasures: all our research so far has not enabled us to produce one. All we can do is to encourage the humans to take the pleasures which our Enemy has produced, at times, or in ways, or in degrees, which he has forbidden."

Screwtape admonishes Wormwood, towards his subject, "Don't waste time trying to make him think that materialism is true! Make him think it is strong or stark or courageous—that it is the philosophy of the future. That's the sort of thing he cares about."

Hell has a hunger that cannot be sated; it is bent on devouring every human soul. Screwtape's sleepless ambition is to possess, consume, and feast upon the tortured spirits of his victims. This is the object of all his machinations. "To us a human is primarily food; our aim is the absorption of its will into ours, the increase of our own area of selfhood at its expense."

Compare all that to the motives of "the Enemy," as admitted by Screwtape. God wants individuals united to him, people remade in his image, yet distinct and fully themselves. They are not seized through force or deception, but rather they exercise the freedom to choose God and the joy of his presence.

"He really does want to fill the universe with a lot of loathsome little replicas of himself—creatures whose life, on its miniature scale, will be qualitatively like his own, not because he has absorbed them but because their wills freely conform to his," Screwtape complains. "We want cattle who can finally become food; He wants servants who can finally become sons."

C.S. Lewis describes Screwtape's (and therefore mammon's) view on property.[7] A sense of ownership, Lewis argues through Screwtape, is one of the main things that leads people into sin. "It is difficult for a man to covet his neighbour's property if he doesn't believe that either he or his neighbour really owns anything." "What men think of as their possessions (including even their bodies and clothes),"

---

7   C.S. Lewis, The Screwtape Letters, 21st letter.

Screwtape tells Wormwood, "are really only things on loan to them from God. Humans are only able to think of things as their property because they have a flawed sense of perspective."

Screwtape further: "The sense of ownership in general is always to be encouraged. The humans are always putting up claims to ownership which sound equally funny in Heaven and in Hell and we must keep them doing so.

It is as if a royal child whom his father has placed, for love's sake, in titular command of some great province, under the real rule of wise counsellors, should come to fancy he really owns the cities, the forests, and the corn, in the same way as he owns the bricks on the nursery floor. We produce this sense of ownership not only by pride but by confusion. We teach them not to notice the different senses of the possessive pronoun 'my' which runs progressively through, 'my boots,' 'my dog,'" 'my servant,' 'my wife,' 'my father,' "my master' and 'my country,' to 'my God.' They can be taught to reduce all these senses to that of 'my boots,' the 'my' of ownership. Even in the nursery a child can be taught to mean by 'my Teddy-bear' not the old imagined recipient of affection to whom it stands in a special relation (for that is what the Enemy will teach them to mean if we are not careful) but 'the bear I can pull to pieces if I like.'"

Screwtape goes on to say, "And all the time the joke is, that the word "Mine" in its fully possessive sense cannot be uttered by a human being about anything."

The real truth as described by Paul, is, in his own words, "As poor, yet making many rich; as having nothing, yet possessing everything."[8] He asked a thought-provoking question; "What do you have that you did not receive?"[9]

"Human ownership is the most productive lie in mammon's repertoire," C.S. Lewis said. "Satan will wreck a lot of men with sexual

---

8   2 Corinthians 6:10
9   I Corinthians 4:7

temptation, but he is far more productive in mammon's speciality area of ownership and greed.

It's not your time, your money, your talent or your body. You may as well lay claim to the moon or the sun. You do not own a single thing."

The early Church Reformer, Ulrich Zwingli said, "Even if we were not sinful by nature, the sin of having private property would suffice to condemn us before God; for that which he gives us freely, we appropriate to ourselves."

Once mammon convinces us that ownership belongs to us, we become selfish in our management and very unkind in our behaviour. As a friend said, "I can get really bent out of shape if you start taking up my time or asking for my money"

When talking about ownership, we must realise that everything belongs to God! Abraham Kuyper, a Dutch theologian started a Christian newspaper, Christian school, a Christian University amongst others, because he believed that Christ should be pre-eminent in all walks of life. He is famously quoted as saying, "There is not a square inch in the whole domain of human existence over which Christ, who is Sovereign over all, does not cry 'Mine!'"

However, C.S Lewis reminded us that the fallen angel Satan, with his Chief Financial Officer, mammon, is actively at work breaking up Christian influence in the world. "There is no neutral ground in the universe; every square inch, every split second, is claimed by God – and counter-claimed by Satan."

The world is a broken kingdom, but still belongs to God – and He wants it back!

There's a nice story told about Pope John XIII, when he was still Venice's Cardinal Roncalli. He was having dinner one night with a priestly assistant who was reporting to the cardinal about another priest, a bit of a renegade, who was doing things that were embarrassing the hierarchy. The future pope listened calmly, sipping wine from a goblet. Finally, the assistant cried out in a frustrated tone, "How can you take this so calmly? Don't you realise what this priest is doing?" The cardinal then gently asked the younger priest, "Father, whose goblet is this?" "It is yours, Your Eminence," the priest answered. The cardinal then threw the goblet to the floor, and it shattered into many fragments. "And now whose goblet is it?" he asked. "It is still yours," was the answer. "And so is this priest still my brother in Christ," said the cardinal with a note of sadness in his voice, "even though he is shattered and broken."

Mammon's temptations

One of the most penetrating songs to have been composed in recent years to describe our consumer culture, in which we are all obsessed with 'purchasing power' is by Shania Twain called, "Ka-Ching". Ka-ching is the sound we used to hear at cash machines after paying for something - music to the ears of the shopkeepers!

The lyrics go …

> We live in a greedy little world
> That teaches every little boy and girl
> To earn as much as they can possibly
> Then turn around and spend it foolishly
> We've created us a credit card mess
> We spend the money that we don't possess
> Our religion is to go and blow it all
> So we're shopping every Sunday at the mall
>
> All we ever want is more
> A lot more than we had before
> So take me to the nearest store
>
> Can you hear it ring
> It makes you wanna sing
> It's such a beautiful thing
> Lots of diamond rings

The happiness it brings
You'll live like a king
With lots of money and things

When you're broke, go and get a loan
Take out another mortgage on your home
Consolidate so you can afford
To go and spend some more when you get bored

Dig deeper in your pocket
Come on, I know you've got it
Dig deeper in your wallet …

We all live in a money hungry world. And if poets, songwriters, and artists are modern day prophets, then this song seems to be making a mockery of money and consumerism. Yet as you listen to the tune, it is quite bright and cheery, perhaps expressing the illusion that money can buy happiness. That's mammon at work!

Paradise Lost

It was the English who first welcomed and established Mammon in early writings. The writer De Plessy — who came after Spenser, (whose 'Faerie Queen' depicts Mammon as overseeing a cave of worldly wealth,) and Milton, (whose 'Paradise Lost' describes Mammon as a fallen angel who values earthly treasure above all things and hence treasures the earth in the wrong way) — called Mammon "Hell's ambassador to England."

In his epic poem "Paradise Lost", John Milton wrote as early as the 17th century about mammon , as one of the fallen angels, and described mammon as 'a devil who always, like a monkey, suffers forwards, searching for treasures on the ground, which should remain hidden...[10]

---

10   Paradise Lost, Book 1, 675-688

"A numerous Brigade hasten'd. As when Bands
Of Pioneers with Spade and Pickax arm'd
Forerun the Royal Camp, to trench a Field,
Or cast a Rampart. Mammon led them on,
Mammon, the least erected Spirit that fell
From heaven, for even in heaven his looks and thoughts
Were always downward bent, admiring more
The riches of Heaven's pavement, trodden Gold,
Then aught divine or holy else enjoyed
In vision beatific; by him first
Men also, and by his suggestion taught,
Ransacked the Center, and with impious hands
Rifled the bowels of their mother Earth
For Treasures better hid."

Mammon is a 'fallen angel', and is hell bent for our addiction.

The poet Lord Byron wrote, "Maidens, like moths, are ever caught by glare, and Mammon wins his way where seraphs might despair."[11] Mammon seems to be winning the battle for hearts and minds leaving the true angels of God in despair!

Our 'monkey' - mammon was there before the beginning of time ... and is still busy with the same aims. He still tries to drag us down with his tricks and illusions.

Money as a Power

The Bible talks of 'principalities and powers[12]' which are among the created beings, made by God for His purposes. The fact that God made and sustains the very enemies that rebel against Him is a mind-boggling reality that may never be fully clear to us. He is the King and has a purpose for everything—even for evil principalities

---

11   Lord Byron, Childe Harold's Pilgrimage, Canto I (1812)
12   Colossians 1:16

and powers[13].

Originally part of God's good creation, these powers have, because of sin, lost their proper relationship to God. They have fallen and are in revolt against their creator. This is why the powers bring with them such mixed results - good and evil, blessing and cursing. This is why Paul can speak of the powers (Greek *exousia*) as both the stabilising forces in the Roman government[14] and the demonic forces we are to wage war against.[15]. The conviction was that behind earthly rulers, social institutions, and many other things were invisible spiritual authorities and powers that were of an angelic or demonic nature.

Money is one of these powers. When Jesus uses the Aramaic term mammon to refer to wealth, he is giving it a personal and spiritual character. When he declares, 'You cannot serve God and mammon,' he is personifying mammon as a rival god. In saying this, Jesus is making it unmistakably clear that money is not some impersonal medium of exchange. Money is not something that is morally neutral, a resource to be used in good or bad ways depending solely upon our attitude toward it. Mammon is a power that seeks to dominate us.

When the Bible refers to money as a power, it does not mean something vague or impersonal. Nor does it mean power in the sense we mean when we speak, for example, of 'purchasing power.' No, according to Jesus and all the writers of the New Testament, behind money are very real spiritual forces that energise it and give it a life of its own. Hence, money is an active agent; it is a law unto itself, and it is capable of inspiring devotion. It is the ability of money to inspire devotion that brings its dark side to the forefront.

Again, in Colossians, we see that principalities and powers have been defeated and shamed by Jesus Christ's work on the cross[16]. They have been disarmed and Jesus "made a public spectacle of them,

---

13   Proverbs 16:4; Daniel 4:35; Isaiah 46:10-11.

14   Romans 13:1

15   Ephesians 6:12

16   Colossians 2:15

triumphing over them by the cross." Satan's goal has always been to steal the affections of mankind from God, and to then destroy God's beloved creation. But Jesus made it possible for all who believe to be reconciled to God—apart from the law, and in spite of any and all sins by which Satan has tempted them[17].

What do these powers do? They separate us from the love of God.

The reason for the complexity of life is not simply the perversity and sin of individual human beings or even the cumulative effect of all the sinners in the world, but something more systemic, something all-embracing. For every visible foreground to a person's life - embracing family, work, community service, leisure, citizenship and church - there is an invisible background that is profoundly influential. We want to do good, to serve God and our neighbour, to do an honest day's work, but we find ourselves confronted with "the system"-with frozen tradition, with intractable institutions, with deeply engrained social patterns that resist us, and, finally, with the world of spiritual beings and forces. What makes life difficult is systemic evil.

The trouble we experience in the world is multifaceted and comes to us through unjust or unloving structures, systems of business and finance, principles of conformity, language and social patterns, customs and traditions that marginalise the life of faith or positively oppose it, and the ever-present influence of the mass media. In addition, there is the world of the spirits. All these are interdependently, systemically resistant to God's purposes in the world and constantly hinder the steps of believers.

Paul deals with the trouble of living in this world through a cluster of terms that include power(s), thrones, authorities, virtues, dominions, names and thrones.[18] These powers are socio-political and spiritual forces, both the outer and the inner structures of life, both the earthly and the heavenly.

---

17   Romans 3:21-28

18   (Romans 8:38; 1 Cor. 15:24; Ephes. 1:21; Ephes. 3:10; Ephes. 6:12; Col. 1:16; Col. 2:10, 15).

A stunning example of how the inner and outer realities of a power are intertwined, and inseparable is the case of money. Mammon is an alternative god; the name Mammon in Aramaic is like our word 'Amen,' which means firmness or stability, something I can trust. It is not surprising that a common English phrase is "the almighty dollar." As Jacques Ellul[19] shows, wealth has some of the pretended claims of deity: (1) it is capable of moving other things and claims a certain autonomy; (2) it is invested with spiritual power that can enslave us, replacing single-minded love for God and neighbour with commercial relationships in which even the soul is bought[20] ; (3) it is more or less personal. So money, "unrighteous mammon," is a form or appearance of another power.[21]

We must recognise the seductive power of mammon. Money has power, spiritual power, to win our hearts. Behind our coins and euro notes, cryptocurrency, or whatever material form we choose to give to our money are spiritual forces.

It is the spiritual reality behind money that we want so badly to deny. For years I felt that Jesus was exaggerating by fixing such a huge gulf between mammon and God. Couldn't we show how advanced we are in the Christian life by giving each his due, God and mammon? Why not be joyful children of the world just as we are joyful children of God? Aren't the goods of the earth meant for our happiness? But the thing I failed to see, and the thing that Jesus saw so clearly, is the way in which mammon makes a bid for our hearts. Mammon asks for our allegiance in a way that sucks the milk of human kindness out of our very being.

That is why so much of Jesus' teaching regarding wealth is evangelistic in character. He calls people to turn away from the mammon god in order to worship the one true God.

For Christ, money is an idolatry we must be converted from in order to be converted to him. The rejection of the god mammon is a

---

19   Power and Money (pp. 76-77, 81, 93)

20   Rev. 18:11-13

21   Ephesians 1:21

necessary precondition to becoming a disciple of Jesus. And in point of fact, money has many of the characteristics of deity. It promises us security, can induce guilt, gives us freedom, gives us power and seems to be omnipresent. Most sinister of all, however, is its bid for omnipotence.

Behind money are invisible spiritual powers, powers that are seductive and deceptive, powers that demand an all-embracing devotion. It is this fact that the apostle Paul saw when he observed that, "The love of money is the root of all evils".[22] Many have rightly observed that Paul did not say, 'money' but 'the love of money.' Given the almost universal love of money, however, they are often the same in practice. Paul saw the same thing Jesus was dealing with in his many statements about money, namely, that it is a god that is out to gain our allegiance. By saying that the love of money is the root of all evils he does not mean in a literal sense that money produces all evils. He means that there is no kind of evil the person who loves money will not do to get it and hold onto it. All restraint is removed; the lover of money will do anything for it. And that is precisely its seductive character; for the person who loves money, no half measures will do. The person is hooked. Money becomes a consuming, life-dominating problem. It is a god demanding an all-inclusive allegiance.

---

22   1 Timothy 6:10

THE MONKEY'S REAL BUSINESS

The monkey's real business is simply attempting to control the world economy; the transactions of which buying and selling. Ultimately, mammon is out to buy the souls of people.

In the Garden

When Eve was tempted by the serpent and had to give an account of what she had done, she explained, "the serpent deceived me ... then I ate"[1] This word 'deceived' in Hebrew comes from a root '*nasha*' which represents a homonym = a word having different meanings. - to deceive, and to lend at interest.

This Hebrew word is strongly linked to the verb '*nashak*' which means to strike with a sting! "Will not your creditors (*nashak*) suddenly arise? Will they not wake up and make you tremble? Then you will become their victim."[2]

Lending at interest is at its root a deceit, tempting people into bondage. Just like the serpent tempted Eve into a bargain of debt which she could never, ever repay. Borrowing money is almost like opening a Pandora's Box, because we never know what is going to happen next! In Greek mythology, the story of Pandora, the first woman, who opens her jar out of curiosity, thereby releasing poverty, hunger and disease into the world, tells the same story as the Bible.

---

1 Genesis 3:13
2 Habakkuk 2:7

According to Greek legend, this first woman, Pandora, was actually sent as a curse to Zeus' men and was given a present upon her marriage. The present was a box that she was told never to open. Needless to say, her curiosity got the better of her (like eating forbidden fruit) and she unleashed eight demons unto the world. The first seven being the seven deadly sins, and the last, which she managed to capture, was hope.

Opening Pandora's box refers to getting into a situation over which one has very little control. Pandora was to be the first of a race of women, the first bride bringing great misery, living with mortal men as companions only in times of plenty, and then to desert them when times became difficult! (Does this sound like a bank?)

Mammon's tricks began at the beginning of Biblical times and have continued throughout history. Debt is one of his main tools with which to enslave people, not just spiritual debt but also material debt, which also enslaves. "The rich rule over the poor, and the borrower is slave to the lender."[3]

Dr. Tomáš Sedláček, Czech economics professor, said in an interview with the German magazine 'Der Spiegel,' "Eve and Adam grab the opportunity and eat the fruit. The original sin has the character of excessive, unnecessary consumption." This sin got us into a debt which was impossible for us to ever pay, under our own resources. It took someone special to be able to pay this debt!

A multinational business

It is claimed that mammon was already present in the commercial and religious vocabulary of the Phoenicians, one of the main trading peoples for more than 600 years BC. The Phoenicians were based in Tyre and descended from the original inhabitants of the promised land - the Canaanites. Ezekiel prophesied the downfall of that once

---

3   Proverbs 22:7

so glorious and mighty trading nation and explained its decline and fall in chapters 26-28 of his book.

The fall of Tyre was poetically described,
> "'How you have perished, you who were inhabited from
> the seas,
> O city renowned, who was mighty on the sea;
> she and her inhabitants imposed their terror on all her
> inhabitants!
> Now the coastlands tremble on the day of your fall,
> and the coastlands that are on the sea are dismayed at
> your passing.'[4]

Tyre, which gathered a tremendous power for that time, imagined itself to be a god and Ezekiel described Tyre as an earthly image of Lucifer, who fell from heaven. His lamentation was:[5]

"You were an anointed guardian cherub. I placed you; you were on the holy mountain of God; in the midst of the stones of fire you walked. You were blameless in your ways from the day you were created, till unrighteousness was found in you. In the abundance of your trade you were filled with violence in your midst, and you sinned; so I cast you as a profane thing from the mountain of God, and I destroyed you, O guardian cherub, from the midst of the stones of fire. Your heart was proud because of your beauty; you corrupted your wisdom for the sake of your splendour. I cast you to the ground; I exposed you before kings, to feast their eyes on you. By the multitude of your iniquities, in the unrighteousness of your trade you profaned your sanctuaries; so I brought fire out from your midst; it consumed you, and I turned you to ashes on the earth in the sight of all who saw you."

This large multinational trading company, Tyre, fell because it was serving money and not God. Mammon was involved in 'violent and corrupt trade'. The unrighteousness of the trading which was going

---

4   Ezekiel 26:17:18
5   Ezekiel 28:16-18

on totally neglected Gods ways of doing business, ignoring the basic principles of trade which God has laid into His creation.

The downfall of the traders who ignored Gods universal principles and followed the path of mammon was ultimate destruction. We cannot constantly and consciously neglect God and escape the consequences.

Prophets, priests and kings

Mammon could even influence prophets, priests and kings! Here are examples of how mammon can get hold of our leaders.

The prophet - Balaam, was hired by King Balak of Moab who sent princes offering money to Balaam in return for him to curse God's people - and Balaam was only too eager to do so. Money was his real god and brought his remarkable career to its end. "They have left the straight way and wandered off to follow the way of Balaam son of Bezer, who loved the wages of wickedness, (*adikia*). But he was rebuked for his wrongdoing by a donkey—an animal without speech—who spoke with a human voice and restrained the prophet's madness."[6]

Love of money was Balaam's downfall. Balaam "loved the wages of unrighteousness" so much that he was used as a prototype of the corruption which money breeds: "Woe unto them! For they...ran greedily after the error of Balaam for reward".[7] Offering spiritual benefits for money is called "the way of Balaam." It prospers in the church today because multitudes are enticed to believe and obey those who promise health and wealth in exchange for a "faith" offering.

The priest - Aaron, substituted the worship of God for a golden idol. Moses had delayed coming down the mountain after forty days and forty nights since Moses left the people to go up the mountain and receive from God his commandments and covenant for them.

---

6   2 Peter 2:15,16
7   Jude 11

Moses' absence created an atmosphere of frightened impatience in the people. They had been delivered from Egypt, defeated an army and crossed the Red Sea, bringing with them huge amounts of gold out of Egypt … and mammon used this to corrupt them!

His words to Moses are remarkable: "I told them (the Israelites) 'Whoever has any gold jewellery, take it off.' Then they gave me the gold, and I threw it into the fire, and out came this calf!"[8]. Voila! Just like that! An extraordinary process if ever there was one. It wasn't a total lie, but Aaron's response certainly was intended to mask the truth and to shift the blame. We know what really happened from several verses earlier: "He (Aaron) took what they handed him and made it into an idol cast in the shape of a calf, fashioning it with a tool" (Exodus 32:4). Aaron built the thing, there's no way around it. Rather than do God's work, he succumbed to the will of those around him.

This was done at the very time when Moses received the commandments; the first two of which were "you shall have no other gods but me and you shall not make idols." Breaking the very 1st. and 2nd. commandments, the Israelites used their God given resource, the gold, and abused its purpose, turning it into their idol, and worshipped it. They served it with their hearts, bodies, and passion. They made it the object of their affection and devotion, they put their trust in it, they rejected the God of Israel who rescued them. Even the first ever priest, was corrupted by gold, making it into an idol and worshipping it. Mammon does not want our gold, but ultimately our worship!

The king – Solomon should have heeded God's warning to the future kings of Israel: "And he shall not acquire many wives for himself, lest his heart turn away, nor shall he acquire for himself excessive silver and gold."[9] King Solomon had all the fame and fortune that any man could achieve or desire. He was the world's wisest and

---

8   Exodus 32:24
9   Deuteronomy 17:17

wealthiest king. And yet, tragically, he threw it all away for the love of money, the pleasures of sex, and the powers of an earthly kingdom. Solomon violated both commands. The prophet Samuel warned the people that the king would take over their wealth and that he would eventually be overcome by the power of wealth[10].

The wealth of Solomon was enormous. The treasure saved for him by David seemed inexhaustible, and the tribute from other peoples,[11] the monopolies granted by the king,[12] the importation of gold from Ophir,[13] etc., brought immense revenues. The king was proportionately extravagant. Read the account given of his palaces, his gardens, and his retinue. No country could long bear such a strain. Increased taxation was necessary, and it was this which brought about the fulfilment of God's word of condemnation against Solomon. Against the advice of his father's wise counsellors, his son Rehoboam decided to impose a very heavy tax burden on his people.[14] This was major a factor leading to the break-up of the kingdom of Israel into two parts.

Mammon was out to snare the prophet, priest and king!

Job

Satan says to God, "Job is just, upright, a man of integrity because he is rich, because you have blessed him." He adds, "If[15] you take away his wealth, Job will stop being righteous." The whole problem is a love problem. What or who does Job love? Wealth or God? We have already seen that we can love only one or the other, that reconciliation of the two is impossible. Job loses his wealth. He has nothing left. And he suffers a violent depression. He rips his coat; he shaves his

---

10   1 Sam 8:10-18
11   1 Kings 10:25
12   1 Kings 10:28, 29
13   1 Kings 9:28
14   1 Kings 12:6-15
15   Job 1:10,11

head. God never forbids us to have human emotions. If Job collapses after losing his wealth and his family, God does not reproach him. But to whom is Job really attached? Will he sink in despair, will he accuse God of being unjust? That is the big question. Is God just when he favours us, makes us rich and blesses us? Is he unjust when he punishes, takes away our possessions and condemns us? Does God have an account to keep with us? Will we accept his judgments only if we understand them?

He sits down and says, "For has anyone said to God, 'I have borne punishment; I will not offend any more; teach me what I do not see; if I have done iniquity (*adikia*), I will do it no more?"[16] When honestly evaluating his motives before God, he asks God if money was his real problem. "If I have put my trust in gold or said to pure gold, 'You are my security,' if I have rejoiced over my great wealth, the fortune my hands had gained.... then these also would be sins to be judged, for I would have been unfaithful to God on high"[17]

Job does not understand what is going on, but Job knows that all he had was really God's, that God can do as he pleases, that he gives and takes away according to his will, and that what counts is communion with him and not the things he gives us for a little while. Job loves God more than God's gifts, and he will not depart from God simply because God takes away everything that made life happy, good and blessed. "Naked I came from my mother's womb, and naked shall I return; the LORD gave, and the LORD has taken away; blessed be the name of the LORD"[18]

What is true of material wealth is also true of spiritual wealth. When his wealth disappeared, Job did not abandon him who is his righteousness. He did not depend on his wealth because he depended on God who was his whole life. It was not enough for him to say, "Naturally, we love God more than our money." He had to prove it. Zechariah even tells us that it is terribly dangerous to say, "Blessed be

---

16   Job 34:31,32
17   Job 31:24,25,28
18   Job 1:21

the LORD, I have become rich"[19] . It is not enough to bless the Lord when one is rich; in fact, this can bring on God's wrath, as the rest of that passage shows.

Mammon was out to send Job into depression and despair at the loss of his wealth; God was out to reinforce Job's dependence on Him so that Job could be even more blessed!

Mammon is out to buy and sell people.

The prophet Amos pronounced judgement on Israel. "Thus says the Lord: For three transgressions of Israel, and for four, I will not evoke the punishment, because they sell the righteous for silver, and the needy for a pair of sandals[20] …" Israel's judges were mercenary and corrupt. They took bribes to condemn the righteous; and even for articles of clothing, such as a pair of shoes, they condemned the poor man, and delivered him into the hands of his creditors.

Amos went on saying, "Hear this, you who trample on the needy and bring the poor of the land to an end, saying, "When will the new moon be over, that we may sell grain? And the Sabbath, that we may offer wheat for sale, that we may make the ephah small and the shekel great and deal deceitfully with false balances, that we may buy the poor for silver and the needy for a pair of sandals and sell the chaff of the wheat?"[21]

When we deal unrighteously with money, people always end up becoming exploited and used for financial gain. Merchants could not wait for the Sabbath to end so that they could start selling again and deceiving their customers by selling inferior products, inflating prices, giving false weights and measures and exploiting their workers.

---

19   Zechariah 11:5
20   Amos 2:6
21   Amos 8:6

Judah

Joseph, as a type of Christ, was sold for the going price of a slave, 20 pieces of silver. His brothers planned to kill him until one of them decided that it would be more profitable to sell him into slavery instead. Judah asks, 'What will we gain if we kill our brother and cover up his blood? Come, let's sell him to the Ishmaelites!" Unlike his brother Reuben, Judah does not spare him simply in hopes of later setting him free; he wants to make a profit. Judah was well and truly under mammon's control!

Ahab & Jezebel

Sometimes we sell our very selves to mammon. We see how Ahab and his wife Jezebel coupled with mammon to get Naboth's vineyard. Naboth owned a vineyard next to the palace of King Ahab at Jezreel. The king offered to buy Naboth's vineyard or exchange it for a better one. Naboth flatly refused. The king returned home to sulk until Queen Jezebel had Naboth convicted on false charges and stoned to death. Ahab seized the vineyard, but the prophet Elijah stepped in to foretell the downfall of Ahab's dynasty. "Ahab said to Elijah, "Have you found me, O my enemy?" Elijah answered, "I have found you, because you have sold yourself to do what is evil (*adikia*) in the sight of the Lord."[22]

Zacchaeus

Zacchaeus was a chief tax collector in Israel, which was a conquered nation, under military occupation. Their conquerors, the Romans, levied oppressive taxes on each colony as a means for transferring most of the nation's wealth and capital to Rome and its citizens. This left people impoverished and subjugated to their rulers. The only people who lived in comfort and ease in Israel were the Romans who ruled and

---

22   1 Kings 21:20

their local collaborators, the tax collectors. Everyone despised them. The incentive the Romans offered tax collectors was almost irresistible. Backed by military force, the tax collector was allowed to demand much more money from his fellow Jews than he had contracted to pay the government. Today, we call this extortion. It was extremely lucrative. Tax collectors were the wealthiest people in society, and the most hated. No wonder the people called him a sinner.[23]

He used his position and love for money to 'sell his people' to the Roman oppressors and keep them enslaved. They were not completely free to conduct their affairs and manage their households and businesses well, due to this excessive tax burden. However, The Holy Spirit moved him to seek out Jesus, who introduced grace into Zacchaeus' life and work. "Zacchaeus stood up and said to the Lord, "Look, Lord! Here and now I give half of my possessions to the poor, and if I have cheated anybody out of anything, I will pay back four times the amount." He began to understand Gods economy which wants to set people free from the burden of mammon!

Ananias & Saphira

In the early church in Jerusalem, a group of believers were so filled with the Holy Spirit that they were of one heart and one mind. They were so committed that they shared all they had so that there was not one needy person. Some even sold land or houses and brought the money to the Apostles. A couple, Ananias and Sapphira decided to sell some property and donate to the cause. However, mammon was firmly rooted in their lives and they lied to God about what they were giving. "Ananias, how is it that Satan has so filled your heart that you have lied to the Holy Spirit and have kept for yourself some of the money you received for the land? Didn't it belong to you before it was sold? And after it was sold, wasn't the money at your disposal? What made you think of doing such a thing? You have not lied just to human beings but to God."[24]

---

23   Luke 19:2
24   Acts 5:3,4

Here, God is setting an example of dealing with mammon right at the very start of the Church. Mammon influence and the deceit it brought needed to be radically expelled! It is an example of how explosively God deals with sin which is exposed to Him directly!

Simon the Magician

Simon, the Magician thought so too, and sold himself to mammon, thinking he could buy the ability to perform the miracles he saw the apostles doing. He had a lucrative business and wanted to expand his product range! He offered the apostles money saying, "Give me this power also, so that anyone on whom I lay my hands may receive the Holy Spirit."[25]

Peter saw right through him, saw mammon at work and rebuked him. "May your silver perish with you, because you thought you could obtain the gift of God with money! You have neither part nor lot in this matter, for your heart is not right before God. Repent, therefore, of this wickedness of yours, and pray to the Lord that, if possible, the intent of your heart may be forgiven you. For I see that you are in the gall of bitterness and in the bond of iniquity (*adikia*)." He was all and truly wrapped up by mammon and demonstrated the wickedness of mammon.

Tertullian, known in early church history as the father of Latin theology, wrote, "Nothing that is God's is obtainable by money."

Babylon

The Bible prophesied that in the end times, mammon will completely control our economy. The spirit of the anti-Christ will not rule by the threat of nuclear war, but the threat of not being able to buy or sell. "Also, it causes all, both small and great, both rich and poor, both free and slave, to be marked on the right hand or the forehead, so that no

---

25 Acts 8:19

one can buy or sell unless he has the mark, that is, the name of the beast or the number of its name."[26]

The term 'Babylon', as used in Revelation is a representative of the world economy and how it represses people whilst living in luxury. Babylon will be judged; "and the merchants of the earth weep and mourn for her, since no one buys their cargo anymore, cargo of gold, silver, jewels, pearls, fine linen, purple cloth, silk, scarlet cloth, all kinds of scented wood, all kinds of articles of ivory, all kinds of articles of costly wood, bronze, iron and marble, cinnamon, spice, incense, myrrh, frankincense, wine, oil, fine flour, wheat, cattle and sheep, horses and chariots, and slaves, that is, <u>human souls.</u>"[27] The buying and selling of human souls is the prophesied destiny of the world economy. Mammon will get the economy completely in his grasp and be able to take complete control over human souls, revelling in their worship.

Jesus in the Temple

One of the most surprising accounts in Jesus' life is for me, when Jesus got so angry in the Temple grounds. "In the temple courts he found people selling cattle, sheep and doves, and others sitting at tables exchanging money. So he made a whip out of cords, and drove all from the temple courts, both sheep and cattle; he scattered the coins of the money changers and overturned their tables. To those who sold doves he said, "Get these out of here! Stop turning my Father's house into a market!"[28]

This was not in character at all. We always have a different picture of Jesus as being kind, patient and loving. Then why was Jesus so angry? The event took place in the Court of the Gentiles – that place in the temple where non-Jews could come to receive grace. Mammon was there taking charge of a marketplace buying and selling where grace should be freely given and received.

---

26   Revelation 13:16,17
27   Revelation 18:11-13
28   John 2:14-16

Jesus approached a temple pulsating with buying and selling. The court of the Gentiles, the place designed all along for foreigners to congregate, for the nations to seek the Lord, was overrun with opportunists trying to turn a profit. And the Jewish leaders had let this happen.

The Pharisees, who controlled the market, did not want Roman money to be used. People wanting to buy some offers for the Temple had to change their currency for temple currency. The Pharisees, who we know loved money, took advantage of the pilgrims and earned money on the currency exchange at inflated rates. Moreover, animals were being offered at high prices. Furthermore, these animals were often second-rate. No wonder Jesus called the place a 'den of robbers.'[29]

The main point, I believe, is that buying and selling has taken the place of giving and receiving. Pilgrims who genuinely wanted to come to the Temple to meet God and to offer sacrifices for atonement of their sons were faced with mammon instead! No wonder Jesus decided to turn the tables! Quoting partly from Isaiah 56, "My house shall be called a house of prayer for all the nations,"

Jesus was confronted with his adversary, mammon who denied people the grace his Father was offering. The economic drive of the Pharisees and their agents had crowded out space for the nations to draw near, and therefore Jesus was driving them out. The great sadness of this scene wasn't so much the rows of product quality and price inflating, but that all this left no room for the Gentiles and outcasts to come to God.

The temple had come under mammon control. Instead of being God's house, it was now under the occupation of a hostile power, not the Pharisees, nor even the Romans, but the spirit of mammon. That is why Jesus was so angry and drove mammon out.

---

29   Matthew 21:13

IN CLOSING...

One of the invitations of Jesus which has impacted me the most is the well-known invitation which Jesus gave to believers in Laodicea. "Behold, I stand at the door and knock. If anyone hears my voice and opens the door, I will come in to him and eat with him, and he with me." I responded to Jesus when I was a 16-year-old teenager after a football tournament in the north of England. Now, over 50 years later, I can testify that he did indeed come into my life and we have enjoyed all these years together!

I have also presented this invitation to many others to accept Jesus into their life and seen some respond.

However, some years ago, I realised that this invitation was given to a group of believers in a city, who were totally deluded as to their financial status, their wealth, their quality of life and their spiritual health!

I visited Laodicea, currently in Turkey, a few years back. It lay between Colossae and Hierapolis on a major trade route and developed a successful commercial life.

The city of Laodicea had no water source of its own. It was dependent on water from the nearby spa town Hierapolis which boasted of hot springs and on Colossae which was blessed with cold water springs. These waters merged and when they got to Laodicea they were lukewarm and tasted rough. Jesus used this to characterise the life and work of the believers in Laodicea, which were, in the view of the then glorified Christ, so bad, they made Him almost nauseous. "So, because you are lukewarm, and neither hot nor cold, I will spit you out of my mouth."[1] The reason was the prideful boasting of the believers who said, "we are rich, prosperous and need nothing!" Jesus replied, "You are wretched, pitiful, poor, blind and naked." What an indictment to those prosperous, rich people! What a challenge for you and I to get our perspective on money and wealth aligned with Christ's perspective!

The counsel Jesus gave to those people was to enter into Gods economy and not measure their performance by the world's economic standards. He echoed the beautiful invitation in Isaiah 55 and said, "Buy from me gold refined in the fire, so you can become rich; and white clothes to wear, so you can cover your shameful nakedness; and salve to put on your eyes, so you can see. Those whom I love I rebuke and discipline. So be earnest and repent."[2]

They had been deceived, by mammon, as to the nature of their wealth and quality of life, and they fell for mammon's lies.

Isaiah's invitation was to "Come, all you who are thirsty, come to the waters; and you who have no money, come, buy and eat! Come, buy wine and milk without money and without cost. Why spend money on what is not bread, and your labour on what does not satisfy? Listen, listen to me, and eat what is good, and you will delight in the richest of fare. Give ear and come to me; listen, that you may live. I will make an everlasting covenant with you, my faithful love promised to David."[3]

How can we buy wine, milk and even gold with no money? Mammon would say that it is ridiculous.

The riches Jesus wants to offer you and I, the treasures of heaven, cannot be achieved using the means of man's economy of buying and

---

1   Revelation 3:16
2   Revelation 3:18,19
3   Isaiah 55:1-3

selling. We must enter into God's economy of giving and receiving.

Then comes the wonderful invitation of Jesus which makes all this possible. To believers, you and I, he says that if we listen to his knocking on the door of our lives, open the door and invite Him in, He will sit down with us, and we can start to plan our financial lives together! Then,[4] my resources, put together with God's are multiplied. Whatever we put into God's hands, he multiplies. The little bit of oil a widow placed into Elijah's hands was multiplied greatly,[5] A little boy's lunch of bread and fish, when placed in Jesus' hands fed thousands with much left over![6] A barren nights fishing raised Peter to despair, but when he placed his boat under Jesus command, the boat almost sank from the weight of fish.[7] These wonderful Biblical examples, however, will fade into insignificance, compared with what happens when God multiples what we have placed into His hands in eternity!

Managing money cannot be found in clever methods, or 'steps-to-success', but in an intimate partnership between the risen Christ and you or I. He will not do what I must do, but we can never do what only He can do. The partnership must be lived out in daily life, in dependence on the One who said, "Keep your lives free from the love of money and be content with what you have, because God has said, 'Never will I leave you; never will I forsake you.'"

Let go … and let God!

---

4   Revelation 3:20
5   2 Kings 4:1-7
6   John 6:9
7   Luke 5:5-7

A Closing Prayer

Sir Francis Drake was an English sea captain who lived from 1540 - 1596. He was the second sailor to circumnavigate the globe. This is his famous prayer, one that it would appear God heard and rewarded. Let's make it ours today and see where God takes us!

Disturb us, Lord, when
We are too pleased with ourselves,
When our dreams have come true
Because we dreamed too little,
When we arrived safely
Because we sailed too close to the shore.

Disturb us, Lord, when
With the abundance of things we possess
We have lost our thirst
For the waters of life;
Having fallen in love with life,
We have ceased to dream of eternity
And in our efforts to build a new earth,
We have allowed our vision
Of the new Heaven to dim.

Disturb us, Lord, to dare more boldly,
To venture on wilder seas
Where storms will show Your mastery;
Where losing sight of land,
We shall find the stars.
We ask you to push back
The horizons of our hopes;
And to push back the future
In strength, courage, hope, and love.
This we ask in the name of our Captain, Who is Jesus Christ.
Amen.

DISCLAIMER

In this book, we have used a lot of Biblical quotations. I have placed them in footnotes, to make the text read easier.

I do hope that I have got all references correctly specified. If not, please ket me know!

After a conference, I received a thank-you note from a speaker who wanted to give a last blessing to our ministry. The meetings had gone very well … or so I thought until getting his letter! He later qualified what he wanted to say, in quoting Acts 20:32. "Now I commit you to the Lord and to the word of His grace which is able to build you up…". However, the verse he actually quoted was Acts 19:32, which says, "The assembly was in confusion: Some were shouting one thing; some another. Most of the people did not even know why they were there!"

Be careful when quoting a Bible reference! After reading this book, I hope Acts 20:32 is true for you, and not 19:32.

Anyway, my professor used to say, "If you cannot convince them, confuse them!" So I win both ways!

Peter J. Briscoe, Leiden, The Netherlands

Please feel free to mail me!
peter@briscoe.com

(Acts 20:32)

FOR FURTHER READING

BOOKS

Bailey, Kenneth. *"Jesus Through Middle Eastern Eyes."* IVP Academic. (2008)

Ellul, Jacques. *"Power and Money."* Marshall & Pickering. (1979)

Foster, Richard. *"Money, Sex and Power."* Harper & Row. (1985)

Ireland, Dennis. *"Stewardship and the Kingdom."* (1992)

Lewis, C.S. *"The Screwtape Letters."* Collins. (1985)

Pitts, Earl and Hill, Craig. *"Wealth, Riches and Money."* Family Foundations. (2001)

Stegemann, Ekkehard W. and Wolfgang Stegemann. "The Jesus Movement: A social History of Its First Century. T & T Clark. (1999)

Welby, Justin, *"Dethroning Mammon."* Bloomsbury, 2017)

Witherington, Ben. *"Jesus and Money."* Brazos Press. (2010)

Zhodiates, Spiros. *"How to Manage Money."* AMG Publishers. (1984)

ARTICLES

"A History Of Recent Interpretation of the Parable of the Unjust Steward," by Denis J. Ireland. Westminster Theological Journal 51 (1989) 293-318.

"And how much do you owe? Take your bill, sit down quickly and write…" (Luke 16:5,6) by Luca Marulli   www.tyndale.cam.ac.uk Tyndale Bulletin 63.2 (2012)

"Honor Restored: New Light on the Parable of the Prudent Steward," by David A. Landry and Ben May. JBL, (2000), pp. 287-309.

"The dishonoured Master," by John S. Kloppenburg. Biblical, Vol. 71, No. 4 (1989), pp. 474-495

"The Parable of the Unjust Steward: A Reexamination of the Traditional View in light of Recent Challenges," by Dave L. Matthewson. JETS 38/1 (March 1995), pp. 29-39

"The Parable of the Prudent Steward and its Lucan Context," by David A. Silva. Criswell Theological Review, 6.2., (1993), pp. 255-268

Compass - finances God's way is a global, non-denominational movement teaching financial discipleship and generosity. The purpose is to serve churches, businesses, ministries, schools and other organisations by providing biblically-based solutions on handling money and possessions. Our vision is to see everyone, everywhere faithfully living by God's financial principles in all areas of their lives.

Global mission

Compass' mission is to help people everywhere to learn, apply and teach Gods financial and business principles. We are looking for three major outcomes.

1. To know Christ more intimately as we trust and obey Him, experiencing Christ at work.

2. To become free from worry, fear, stress and anxiety and then be free to serve and love the Lord and our neighbours.

3. To contribute to fulfilling the Great Commission by giving our money and other resources to fund the work of the Church.

The Compass Global Team is comprised of local leadership on 6 continents – Europe, Asia, South America, North America, Africa and the Indian sub-continent. Our continental offices serve more than 90 nations around the world.

Resources

Compass has developed a wide range of resources in a wide variety of formats, such as DVD based teaching, workshops, small group studies, e-books and online learning.

There are teaching resources for all ages, from small children through students to adults; with application to areas of life such as business, church, marriage and family. Compass is active in over 80 nations over the globe and has resources in many languages. Contact our continental offices at www.compass1.org

To see specific English language resources, please visit the US shop at www.compass1.org or the EU shop at www.compass1.eu

Bible Study - THE CHOICE

The study will explain how managing money is a spiritual discipline and will lead you into discovering Biblical truths about being a good and faithful steward of what God has given us to manage.

Managing money is not just a technical exercise, but a spiritual discipline. There is an active power behind money which Jesus unmasked and called 'mammon.' He told his followers in strong terms that, "You cannot serve both God and Mammon."

This Bible study in 5-parts will lead you to discover some answers to questions like:

- Who or what is mammon?
- How does mammon affect our financial decisions?
- How can the influence of mammon be overcome?
- How can we use our money in a way that God would want us to?

9 789083 228563